Christian
Responsibility
in a Hungry World

Christian Responsibility in a Hungry World

C. Dean Freudenberger
Paul M. Minus, Jr.

ABINGDON
Nashville

CHRISTIAN RESPONSIBILITY IN A HUNGRY WORLD

Copyright © 1976 by Abingdon

Library of Congress Cataloging in Publication Data

Freudenberger, C   Dean, 1930-
  Christian responsibility in a hungry world.
  Bibliography: p.
  1. Food supply. 2. Church and social
problems—United States. I. Minus, Paul M.,
joint author. II. Title.
HD9000.5.F74   261.8′5   75-43764

ISBN 0-687-07567-X

MANUFACTURED BY THE PARTHENON PRESS AT
NASHVILLE, TENNESSEE, UNITED STATES OF AMERICA

Contents

CHRISTIAN RESPONSIBILITY IN A HUNGRY WORLD

Introduction

Never before have so many suffered so much from hunger. During the 1970s hunger has preyed especially upon the very young and the elderly, weakening the body's defenses against disease and stunting physical and mental growth. At least 10 million persons (and possibly twice that number) died in 1975 as a direct result of receiving too little food. Today 500 million men, women, and children bear severe and often irreversible effects of malnutrition. Over one-half of the human race exists in conditions of chronic poverty that keep them underfed and uncertain about their next meal. Growing numbers are convinced that their plight need not be so desperate— that if the earth's resources were justly utilized, there would be food for all. They hunger for bread and justice.

This book addresses the more than 100 million Christians in the affluent USA who constitute a sizable portion of the world's well-fed minority. Many American Christians have begun to hear the cry of the hungry and to ask how they should respond. They know that our nation has worked resourcefully to allow men to walk on the moon: now what must be done to provide people the nourishment they need to walk on the earth? No question is more important, for increasingly it is evident that the world's future will be largely determined by what the well-fed minority does about the fact that most of the human family is hungry.

Among the alternative courses of action that compete for our commitment, two are especially tempting. The first urges us to conserve our dwindling abundance for future generations of Americans rather than to squander it upon the millions who appear doomed to starvation. The second urges us to attempt to feed the hungry in this land and abroad through a portion of our surplus wealth. As alluring as these proposals are, we dare accept neither. The reasons for this judgment will become fully evident in the pages that follow. For now, it is enough to say that the first alternative overlooks the fact that constructive steps *can* yet be taken to eradicate hunger around the world, and the second underestimates *how much* these steps will require of the affluent minority.

The authors propose a third alternative that takes account both of the gravity of the hunger crisis and of the hopeful signs marking a road through the crisis toward a future in which there is bread and justice for all. We believe that ample evidence supports the conviction that *such a future can be reached by the end of this century if responsible, persistent effort begins today.*

Christians have no more urgent mission than to make haste along this road and to summon others to the same journey. Times of arduous travel await these modern-day pioneers, for they will be challenged to new and more responsible understandings, priorities, and levels of sharing. But no better means exist to build up the well-being and solidarity of the human family, as well as to liberate the affluent from perilous notions about themselves and the world. In this volatile age, failure to embark immediately and boldly upon this journey may well bring rich and poor alike to a degree of misery worse than any experienced before.

Our exploration of the way to a hunger-free future has been undertaken in the spirit of Martin Buber's words: *"The greater the crisis becomes, the more earnest and consciously responsible is the knowledge demanded of us; for although what is demanded is a deed, only the deed which is born of knowledge will help to overcome the crisis."* Buber's words remind us that the search for deeds able to move the hungry world to a better future must pass through the discipline of acquiring sound knowledge about the present crisis.

We have written this book because we know that growing numbers of Christians want an incisive, comprehensive analysis of world hunger coupled with an indication of what they can do that will genuinely contribute to its conquest. Our book speaks directly to both needs. Part 1 establishes the foundation of knowledge upon which responsible Christian action must be based. That knowledge is drawn from two sources. One is a sociological analysis of hunger's multiple dimensions and of strategies designed to end hunger; the other is biblical wisdom about the human family's quest for food and justice. Part 2 proposes guidelines for churches that are ready to become involved in building a world in which no person is deprived of adequate nourishment.

We realize that a small book dealing with so large and complex a theme cannot possibly answer all the questions that rise in the minds of thoughtful readers. Consequently, we hope that those wishing to know more and reflect further will make use of the resources listed on pages 125-28. There, too, are the addresses of some of the hunger-fighting groups discussed in Part 2; we hope that interested readers will want to be in touch with them. We also realize that our views on controversial issues treated here will not satisfy everyone. But we hope that what we say will cause those who disagree with us at least to take another look at their understanding of world hunger and at their response to it.

The perspectives presented in these pages result from a mingling of the authors' experience in the realms of agronomy, political action, parish ministry, and theological education. We are grateful to the many persons from whom we have learned across the years and around the world. Our seminary co-workers in California and Ohio have been especially helpful to us in the preparation of this volume. We want also to acknowledge our indebtedness and appreciation to the individuals and groups who have allowed us to report their experiences in Part 2.

With more gratitude than can be adequately expressed, we dedicate this book to Elsie and Nancy.

PART 1

Knowledge Required
for a Time of Crisis

Since 1975 the hunger crisis has become somewhat less
severe in several areas of the world because of improved
weather patterns. But this is only a temporary reprieve.
The more fateful fact is that the problem intensifies
quietly each day. The underlying forces that breed
poverty and hunger remain unchecked.

In Part 1 of this book we shall seek to understand the
reasons for this long-range crisis and the changes needed
to overcome it. The first chapter poses the question of
what must be done about the fact that over one-hundred
nations suffer chronic food deficits at the very moment in
history when a handful of affluent nations—ours most
prominent among them—has reached the highest peaks of
material abundance. The second chapter examines the
multiple causes of hunger. The third chapter explains the
steps that will facilitate rural community development
and adequate agricultural production in the food-deficit
nations, and the fourth chapter searches for biblical light
to help us understand the basis and scope of our
responsibility in a hungry world.

CHAPTER 1

The Deadly
but Conquerable Foe

Americans can still escape the grim sight of hunger, but the passing of each month makes it more difficult to do so. Chronic hunger exists in every part of our nation. It is even more pervasive outside the United States. Any open-eyed traveler to Asia, Africa, or Latin America quickly discovers how relentlessly and devastatingly hunger stalks the human family. Over half of the world's population is intimately acquainted with it. These persons know hunger not as a statistic but as the deadly foe of body and spirit.

Nutritionist Alan Berg gives us a glimpse of hunger's human toll: "The light of curiosity absent from children's eyes. Twelve-year-olds with the physical stature of eight-year-olds. Youngsters who lack the energy to brush aside flies collecting about the sores on their faces. Agonizingly slow reflexes of adults crossing traffic. Thirty-year-old mothers who look sixty." [1]

And there is a toll not so readily visible: the grief borne by the victims' loved ones; the permanent mental stunting of millions of children who did not receive adequate protein during the critical early years of brain formation; and the despairing conclusion of young and old alike that poverty has locked them into a joyless struggle from which there is no rescue.

For tragically large numbers of human beings the only escape from hunger is death. It comes among persons whose bodies receive insufficient numbers of calories and then begin to consume their own protein for energy. *Time* magazine describes what happens:

The victim of starvation burns up his own body fats, muscles and tissues for fuel. His body quite literally consumes itself and deteriorates rapidly. The kidneys, liver and endocrine system often cease to function properly. A shortage of carbohydrates, which play a vital role in brain chemistry, affects the mind. Lassitude and confusion set in, so that starvation victims often seem unaware of their plight. The body's defenses drop; disease kills most famine victims before they have time to starve to death. An individual begins to starve when he has lost about a third of his normal body weight. Once his loss exceeds 40%, death is almost inevitable.[2]

Hunger is the human family's most devastating foe, but it is also the most conquerable. Adequate technical knowledge, ethical wisdom, and economic resources exist today to overcome hunger within two decades—*if these assets are put to immediate, informed, and sustained use.* The critical question is this: Does the well-fed world have the will to engage in this battle? And more especially: Shall we affluent Americans make the necessary commitment of ourselves to the battle?

For those persons ready to join the growing ranks of hunger-fighters there are certain kinds of knowledge with which we must be armed. If we know what recent and past processes have produced the current crisis, we shall be in a position to begin to identify the targets for our corrective action. We must feed those who hunger; even more crucially, we must change the processes that will, if unchecked, produce more and more hungry people for years to come.

THE IMMEDIATE PAST

In the early 1970s adverse weather conditions affected crops in the Soviet Union, China, India, Australia, Sahelian Africa, and South Asia, creating unusually heavy worldwide food deficits and high prices for food everywhere. This marked the first serious decline in food production in twenty years. Wheat reserves in the main exporting nations fell to the lowest point reached since World War II. Soaring food prices contributed further to global inflation and placed nineteen nations in the perilous predicament of not being able to purchase food.

During this period of shortage, an aggressive short-term economic boom occurred in the United States and other developed nations, leading to spiraling demands for food and feed grain, and to consequent secret and speculative market activities. Wheat prices rose from an average range of $1.35 to $2.00 per bushel to over $5.00. With dwindling food reserves and inflationary prices facing the United

States and other developed nations, food aid programs to hungry Third World nations were cut.

Compounding the nearly 130 food-deficit nations' difficulty in feeding their people has been the steady erosion of prices for their raw material exports to developed nations and the drastic increase of costs for the scarce fuel and fertilizer they need to produce food.

THE PRE-CRISIS YEARS

The crisis of the 1970s has erupted out of problems that have been accumulating for years and even centuries. We shall now quickly note some of the underlying problems that have been progressively worsening for the last twenty years.

(1) During much of this period, although food production increased, food demand ran ahead of supply by about 0.7 percent a year because of growing population and mounting affluence.

(2) Increased demand for food has reduced the level of international food trade, for many of the former food-exporting nations have placed embargoes on food exports.

(3) In some nations, farmers' incentives for food production have been destroyed, leading farm families to migrate to already crowded cities and hastening the decline of rural, food-growing areas.

(4) The growth rate of global agricultural production has slowed ominously. Among the reasons for this are the difficulty of developing new agricultural projects on

remaining marginal lands; the length of time necessary for producing new plant varieties; the resistance to change among most farmers; and the fact that upwards of a billion farmers must go about their daily work weakened by hunger.

THE OUTLOOK FOR THE FUTURE

What do present facts suggest for the future? World food demand is estimated to increase at the rate of 2.4 percent per year. Two percent will result from population growth, and the remainder from rising affluence and the resulting desire for more food. These are average figures. In the developing countries of Asia, Africa, and Latin America the need for additional food will be significantly higher: an increase of 3.7 percent annually will be necessary simply to keep pace with demand. However, during the past decade their average annual increase has been only 2.7 percent. If their increase does not accelerate to the necessary figure, experts estimate an annual grain deficit of from 85 million to 120 million tons per year by 1985 (compared with a 16 million ton annual deficit for the years between 1969 and 1972).

How can the nations meet their expanding food needs? Faced with sky-rocketing costs and already struggling economies, the majority of the grain-importing food-deficit nations will simply not be able to finance food imports from the few food-exporting nations. Clearly the directions affirmed by the 1974 U.N. World Food Conference must be followed. The way forward for the food-deficit nations is to end their reliance upon food from outside *by rapidly developing their own food-producing capacities.*

Such rural/agricultural development is both necessary and possible. The world community possesses the wealth, agricultural skills, soil management abilities, personnel, and other resources necessary for this task. At present, development programs in the rural/agricultural sector require about $5 billion annually. But these programs are far from adequate. Were the nations to accept the World Food Conference's urgent recommendation that they reduce their spending for military arms by 10 percent (a reduction that would produce a sum of nearly $30 billion), and were they to commit that amount annually for rural and agricultural development over the next twenty years, the world would be well on its way to ending the food-deficit problem in every nation.[3]

Furthermore, the recent experience of such nations as Taiwan and South Korea indicates that meeting nutritional and other elementary human needs would bring a substantial reduction to world population growth. Parents whose families are healthy and decently fed are not under pressure to produce large numbers of children (a point to which we shall return). If such needs are met it should be possible by the end of the century to stabilize world population at approximately seven billion persons, with each of them able to expect a life of sufficiency and dignity.

But time is of the essence. With world population growing exponentially at the current rate of a 73-million increase per year and with other problems intensifying daily, we have only a very short period in which to make the necessary decisions about national priorities and to begin the necessary investment of funds, imagination, and human energies.

Such a reordering of priorities and conversion of funds is within reach of the human family. The great bulk of the world's wealth is controlled by a relatively few nations. The United States could play a leading role in the quest for a hunger-free world. Our amount spent for armaments ($85 billion in 1975) gives us an overkill capacity far beyond our legitimate defense needs. Our average per capita income surpasses the average income of 95 percent of the world's population. Average income in this country is 50 times that of India, 100 times that of Bangladesh. We constitute 5 percent of the world's population but consume nearly ⅓ of its energy and minerals. We produce far more of the world's food than any other nation. Our material abundance gives us a unique opportunity to lead the way in making the national and personal commitments that must come if world hunger is to be conquered.

So far American rhetoric has outpaced American performance. But this can change. There is still time for an all-out effort, and the churches can do much to precipitate it.

If history remembers our country in a kindly light, it will not be because we were first in the number of missiles, cars, and television sets—it will be because in the late 1970s we decided as a people that we cared enough about the world's hungry masses and our common destiny to commit a generous portion of our resources to the task of helping all the nations feed themselves.

CHAPTER 2

Causes of Hunger

The present food crisis has also been produced by certain long-term processes that we must identify if our corrective deeds are to be on target. The underlying causes of hunger are numerous, but ten stand out as deserving special attention.

Our temptation often is to reduce difficult problems to dimensions that are small and simple enough to allow us to imagine that we have established some degree of control over them. But yielding to this temptation leads both to faulty analysis and to simplistic responses. We cannot blame the world hunger crisis upon any one cause or any one group. Nor are there any easy solutions to this crisis. Many things have contributed to it. Hence we must design strategies of response that take all the pertinent factors into account.

(1) *The Colonial Legacy.* Four hundred years of colonialism (especially the last seventy-five years) have contributed much to the emergence of hunger and famine. Colonial systems created agricultural industries for the production of rubber, cocoa, tea, coffee, cotton, vegetable

oils, timber, sugar, and spices. Such industrial crops were useful for the colonial powers, but they did not feed their producers. Today non-food crops form the basis of the economies of food-deficit nations that have become independent since the end of World War II. It is extremely difficult, many times impossible, for these young nations to make rapid agricultural transitions from industrial to food crops.

History also has seen the introduction of crops from the northern temperate zones into the tropical and monsoon regions. Such annual crops as corn, sorghum, millet, peanuts, and cotton never should have been cultivated on a wholesale basis in ancient soils with highly weathered mineral content, exposed to high temperatures and pounding tropical rainfall.

Colonialism has moreover left the hungry nations with a wide gap between landed and serf classes. A few people are very rich, the majority very poor. Generally speaking, colonialism did not make possible the formation of adequate numbers of national leaders. In the vacuum left by departing colonial administrators came self-appointed military leaders with their own priorities and abilities— most of which are not useful for the development of environmentally harmonious, food-producing industries. One of the major legacies of colonial history is a hungry world in the latter decades of the twentieth century.

(2) *Resource Abuse.* Another basic cause of hunger is resource abuse. One merely needs to consider the losses in the midwestern United States during the early 1930s to

understand the effects of destruction in wide areas of Africa, in Central India, and across the major archipelagoes of the Pacific. Land, forest, water, and soil resource loss is related to ignorance and social neglect. Nor can we overlook the ruthless profit motives which have led many corporations to irresponsible agricultural resource destruction such as the burning of range lands in Central Africa and the extraction of timber in the equatorial nations. Internationally, there are too few environmental controls in operation. Many industrial firms take advantage of this situation beyond their own national borders. As consumption patterns rapidly grow in the wealthy nations, their far-flung industrial giants exert damaging impact upon soil, forest, and grassland resources around the world, thus further diminishing the earth's capacity for food production.

(3) *Complexity of Agricultural Development.* Hunger also exists because of the tremendous complexity of raising livestock and food crops within areas which must contend with tropical and monsoon climates and soil zones. Temperatures and humidity are high, as is the incidence of insect and pathogenic pests. Bacterial decomposition rapidly destroys essential organic matter in the soil. Rainfall is high; so is erosion and leaching of soil, with the consequent difficulty of accumulating plant nutrients in the soil.

Another reason for the infertility of these soils is the fact that they are very ancient. They were never removed and re-established by the movements of polar ice caps during

23

the Ice Age. Indeed, the lush green of the equatorial world is a massive disguise for impoverished soil. We need to be constantly aware of these kinds of obstacles facing our international neighbors. It is virtually impossible for new Third World nations to go it alone. Economic and political leaders must come to realize this fact.

(4) *False Assumptions.* Americans have made two basic assumptions that are crippling our response to the world food crisis. The first is the assumption that temperate-zone agricultural technologies can be transferred to the tropical and monsoon world. Annual grain crops, plows, cattle ranching, annual burning, fallow and crop rotation systems, fertilizer, and irrigation are usually not advantageous in those areas. In fact, too often they are detrimental. The second false assumption is that we must increase *our* production to *feed* hungry, food-deficit nations. Increasing U.S. production may be appropriate in the short run, for it does help supply food relief to the hungry nations in emergencies. But we allow this "band-aid" approach to the problem to permeate our thinking and shape national policy toward the developing nations. Hunger will never be overcome until all the food-deficit nations (with the exception of a few whose desert or polar conditions make it physically impossible) are able to produce a sufficient food supply within their own borders.

(5) *Low Status for Agricultural Development.* The extremely low value that economic and political decision-makers have placed upon agriculture and upon

rural community development through the years has contributed to hunger. Persons who have worked to overcome food deficits and malnutrition have constantly cried out for a high priority for agricultural development. But the cries have fallen on deaf ears. The burden of significant research in tropical agriculture has been borne by pioneering programs of foundations and universities. Unfortunately there are no creative government parallels to the private institutes working with rice production in the Philippines, with dwarf wheats and high-lysine maize varieties in Mexico, with lateritic (hard, bricklike) soil and grassland management in Colombia, and with tubers and mixed farming systems in Nigeria. One chronic problem in agricultural development is that decisions about agriculture and rural development are made in national capitals by urban-oriented economic and political leaders. Their orientations and biases inevitably shape priorities and programs for food production. A comparable urban orientation of church leadership has impaired its effectiveness in dealing with hunger and with rural problems.

(6) *Recent Business Expansion.* The economic boom in the developed nations since the 1950s has created historically unprecedented demands on natural resources and food supplies. This has resulted in fuel, fertilizer, and grain shortages, to mention but three major resources. There are, indeed, limits to growth. No one is sure of the parameters. We now are aware, at least, that imbalanced growth often results in empty storage bins which are unable to ensure against inevitably shifting and of-

25

tentimes devastating weather patterns. We know, too, that the consumption and waste habits of the developed nations raise crucial moral issues for our time.

(7) *The Dearth of Agricultural and Rural Community Leadership.* Another serious cause of hunger is the short supply of rural and agricultural leaders in the Third World nations. Colonial regimes trained indigenous personnel primarily to be governmental and industrial leaders, and producers of non-food agricultural products. Agricultural leaders who did receive training received it in the temperate zones of the world, or in the tropics under the tutelage of temperate-zone oriented teachers. This fact, together with the low status and meager salaries given agricultural leaders has resulted in a scarcity of indigenous agronomists, plant geneticists and pathologists, entomologists, veterinarians, agricultural economists, rural sociologists, rural educators, and village extension assistance officers.

(8) *The Arms Race.* Another powerful cause of hunger is the global commitment to arms purchases and military preparedness. Extremely high percentages of expendable national wealth are committed annually among all nations to the maintenance and expansion of military might. Arms sales from manufacturers in the industrialized world doubled during 1975. The nations of the world are now spending more than $275 billion annually for armaments. No wonder there is military violence. No wonder there is inadequate agricultural research and leadership, limited food supplies, and low demand for

rural and agricultural development. One cannot travel anywhere in the world without meeting the tragic simultaneous growth of military might and chronic hunger.

As Americans we must recognize that our economy rests largely upon the military-industrial complex, and upon grain sales to nations unable to produce enough food for themselves. We must be sobered by this reality. We are beginning to hear that our country's key source of international power is the combination of our military might and our ability to control the flow of food and feed grains to most of the nations. That combination gives the United States awesome power. But what responsibility does it place upon us?

(9) *Aid Disenchantment.* International assistance programs from the high-income nations to the food-deficit nations have hit a new low. International aid represents an average of only 0.4 percent of the gross national product of the economically prosperous nations. The aid that is available is not effectively related in any proportionately significant way to the overwhelming problems of hunger and famine. The United States' foreign economic aid represents 1/5 of 1 percent of our Gross National Product and only a small fraction of our defense budget and military assistance programs to the nations. This country, the most wealthy in the world, has dropped to 15th on the list of the 17 major donor nations engaged in development assistance to Third World nations.

As later chapters will indicate, there is a restlessness

among Americans about our present role in the world. A willingness to make a fresh start is emerging. That mood must be nurtured and given articulate leadership. Our people must be helped to move beyond the assumptions of the post–World War II reconstruction period, beyond the mind-set that measured development almost exclusively in terms of GNP and per capita average income increases—beyond that to a new sensitivity that measures aid in terms of achieving justice and increasing life quality for the poorest of the poor.

(10) *Population Growth.* Rapid population growth is *a* cause of world hunger, but it does not play the decisive causal role that many Americans assume. In fact, hunger helps to accelerate the population explosion. As the 1974 United Nations World Population Conference rightly perceived, rapid population increase is a consequence of poverty, social and economic neglect, exploitation, and environmental degeneration. Poor parents produce large numbers of offspring because they know that their life conditions will allow only a few to survive. They want those children because of the joys they can bring, and because of the help they (especially sons) can give in ekeing out a living for the family and in providing for the parents in old age.

Today the population explosion and the affluence explosion together are creating a demand for food that is outrunning the production of food. Clearly population growth must be ended if a hunger-free future is to be reached. The way toward population stabilization has been carefully studied by William Rich. His findings are significant:

In a number of poor countries, birth rates have dropped sharply despite relatively low per capita income and despite the relative newness of family planning programs. The common factor in these countries is that the *majority* of the population has shared in the economic and social benefits of significant national progress to a far greater degree than in most poor countries—or in most Western countries during their comparable periods of development. Appropriate policies for making health, education, and jobs more broadly available to lower income groups in poor countries contribute significantly toward the motivation for smaller families that is the prerequisite of a major reduction in birth rates. Combining policies that give special attention to improving the well-being of the poor majority of the population with large-scale, well-executed family planning programs should make it possible to stabilize population in developing countries much faster than reliance on either approach alone.[1]

A TIME FOR HOPE

We know that none of the causes of hunger can be changed overnight. They have deep roots in social custom and in human nature. But we know, too, that countervailing forces are at work bringing change in each of these ten areas. A novel and promising fact about life in the late twentieth century is the speed with which we move out of the past into the future. The future is pressing upon us, and the task of responsible men and women is to look discerningly for those paths leading beyond the present to a future capable of improving the human condition. John Gardner gives wise counsel:

There are many whose impulse to constructive action is too deeply rooted to be touched by the current fashion of despair. They may know how difficult it is to better the lot of men . . . but they intend to do what they can. If there is a long chance that we can replace brutality with reason, inequity with justice, ignorance with enlightenment, we must try. And our chances are better if we have not convinced ourselves that the cause is hopeless. All effective action is fueled by hope.[2]

CHAPTER 3

Structures and Processes for Rural Development

If we effectively address the causes of hunger, we shall prepare the way for a hunger-free future. But more is necessary to get food out of the ground! For that to happen, the processes of agricultural and rural community development must be initiated in the food-deficit nations. As we have seen, these processes are extremely complex, particularly in the tropical and monsoon regions where soils and climates are so difficult to contend with.

Agricultural and rural development requires informed effort in both the food-deficit nations and the affluent nations. The one group is the place where the development must occur, and the other is the essential source of the resources and the changes needed to undergird it.

IN THE FOOD-DEFICIT NATIONS

People living in rural areas are the principal producers of the world's food supply. Special attention must be directed to rural families in the food-deficit nations if these nations are to be able to feed themselves.

The word "rural" describes the countless millions of people living beyond the sounds and lights of the cities, who are found in remote villages, barrios, and longhouses in or near the earth's deserts, plains, rivers, and forests. In general, rural people are scattered, isolated, and out of contact with one another. Communications are difficult and costly. Social amenities are few. This is the condition of from 60 to 95 percent of the population of each food-deficit nation.

Rural development involves the initiation of many social, economic, political, and religious processes that together can make human life more human for such people. The goal of these activities is to make possible the fulfillment of personal and community potential in harmony with the natural environment of the soil, subsoil, forests, grasslands, wildlife, water, and atmospheric resources of creation. The fulfillment of human potential takes place when there is freedom from the violence of hunger, poverty, ignorance, suspicion, prejudice, and exploitation. Fulfillment of human potential comes when persons are free to make choices about their own future, with self-respect and with a sense of responsibility for the well-being of their neighbors. There is no justice or dignity when there is no possibility for free choice and no concern for the welfare of other persons.

What makes possible the development of rural community and agricultural production among these millions?

The rural community and agricultural development process stands on three legs. It is like a tripod. If one leg is missing, it will fall. The three components necessary for the furthering of rural and agricultural development are farmer justice, rural life support structures, and farmer knowledge about agriculture and the environment.

(1) *Farmer Justice.* Rural and agricultural development requires just use and control of land. Glaring examples of injustice now exist worldwide. We occupy a limited and fragile planet, where by 1985 all arable lands will be cultivated and our present population will have expanded by another billion persons. Movement toward such a future raises crucial questions about the use and ownership of land and other resources. How shall we understand, for example, the just use of all resources? How far shall we go to contest the right of a person or an industrial corporation to destroy or degrade everyone's air resources by polluting them? What about the rights of land use, and the irresponsible abuse of soil resources—resources which have severe limitations and which affect the life of all creatures?

Other issues affecting farmer justice increasingly press themselves upon a world seeking to free itself of hunger. There can be no rural development, for example, if justice is not done for the farmer in the marketplace, within the tax structures, and in the welfare services of a nation. There can be no rural development if there is military conflict with its wanton destruction of agricultural resources. There can be no development if farm people are unable to represent themselves in government arenas and

33

to make needed decisions for themselves and their communities.

But beyond the need for farmer justice, there are other equally essential issues. For example, some people do have land and are free from the fear of military plunder. They do have a chance in the marketplace. Yet, they show little progress toward rural community and agricultural development. That is because other factors are missing.

(2) *Rural Life Support Structures.* Rural development that leads to food production depends on a wide range of physical resources: roads, bridges, markets, credit unions, supplies (such as seed, fertilizer, appropriate pesticides), animal breeding stock, fencing, various forms of farm power, appropriate tools, and community and regional irrigation and drainage systems. Also needed are quarantines to govern the careful movement of livestock and plant parts, and laws about resource use. Essential social services are needed such as public health and educational opportunities, along with organizations allowing just and free political participation. The list goes on to include almost forty essential parts of the rural development puzzle.

The local farm is like a cell in the body. It requires support systems to keep it alive, and it produces essential life-giving energy for the health of the whole body. It likewise requires systems to carry its products wherever they are needed.

One of the first tasks for rural developers in any nation is to understand the complex, interrelated components affecting simultaneously the fashioning of local agricultural, political, environmental, and economic support structures. Assessments of the local situation from all these angles are needed in order to pinpoint missing but essential structures. Such assessments help to identify bottlenecks in the development process. When a bottleneck is spotted (such as the lack of credit facilities, of improved seed stock, or of appropriate tools), effective planning can take place. The bottleneck can be eliminated, and the development process can move forward.

Farmer justice and essential support structures must be complemented by the third leg of the tripod.

(3) *Farmer Knowledge About Food Production and the Environment.* Approximately two thirds of the world's population are rural. Agricultural activity is extremely complex everywhere—even in a kitchen garden in the U.S.A.! One can scarcely imagine its compounded complexity for people in tropical and monsoon regions who must face the difficult conditions already described.

Traditional subsistence agricultural practices sustained as many as one billion persons in 1850. These practices continued to provide the vast majority of food needed to sustain an expanding world population that grew from 1 billion to 3 billion between 1850 and 1960. Now that we are a human family of over 4 billion members (in less than 30 years we shall reach 7.1 billion), traditional agriculture—which typically required years of fallow between crops—just will not work. The farm family has no place to go when soil needs rest or is totally exhausted.

By 1985, all arable land will be occupied. Furthermore, due to the intensification of traditional agricultural practices by a growing rural population, the world's soil resources are being eroded and depleted at alarming rates. Most tragically, very little reliable technical knowledge exists about soil management, food crops, and livestock in the tropics.

How, then, can agricultural development take place when people do not adequately know how to maintain the fertility of their soil, or how to manage their grasslands, forests, and water resources? How can agricultural development take place when people do not adequately know how to keep their poultry alive, economically feed their pigs, effectively grow their fruits and vegetables, graze their cattle, and safely store their grain, tuber, and fiber crops?

If agricultural development is to overcome the changed conditions brought upon us in these latter decades of the twentieth century, it must be built upon a massive effort leading to the acquiring and applying of reliable agricultural and environmental knowledge.

IN THE AFFLUENT NATIONS

The task of the affluent, industrialized nations is to supply the assistance necessary for adequate food production to occur in the food-deficit nations. Most needed is help in establishing processes leading to farmer justice, rural life support systems, and farmer knowledge. Immediate as well as long-range assistance is required.

An instrument capable of effectively channeling such assistance was created by the United Nations World Food Conference in November 1974. Called the World Food Council, this organization serves as the principal mechanism in the world today through which the food-sufficient, wealthy nations can work cooperatively to help the food-deficit nations establish the processes that will enable them to feed themselves.

The World Food Council is composed of 36 nations (the United States included), and it has three principal tasks.

First, the wealthy, industrialized nations are asked to contribute to the International Agricultural Development Fund. Minimum projections are for a budget of five billion dollars a year. The Fund will be used for agricultural research in all the food-deficit nations; for training of agricultural and rural community leaders; for the development of land, forest, and grassland resources; for construction of grain drying and storage facilities; for rural transportation systems; and for making available to rural people such agricultural supplies as fuel, fertilizer, seed, and livestock. Rural public health and educational services also will be provided by the Fund.

Will the governments of the affluent nations contribute enough to allow this Fund to achieve its crucial goals? Clearly, the churches have a role in helping to generate the will and the political decisions necessary to launch the Fund successfully.

Second, the World Food Council plans to create a world-wide emergency food relief program. This consists of an Early Warning Information System, a World Food-Grain Reserve, and a Food Aid Program. The information system will enable the nations to predict pockets of famine by monitoring areas of flood, drought, crop damage or destruction due to infestations of insects and plant diseases. The grain reserve, estimated at between 10 and 60 million metric tons, will assure the delivery of sufficient foodstuffs when there is a threat of severe malnutrition and famine. Careful mechanisms for food aid can be established that do not destroy local farmer incentives and that do not hamper existing reliable food delivery systems.

Here, too, the churches have a role in fostering commitment to a program based on elementary human need rather than the profit motive or national advantage.

Third, the World Food Council is calling upon industrialized nations to cooperate with the raw-material producing nations to create economic processes that will provide steady and appreciable incomes for all. These processes are intended to compensate for the irregularities in climatic patterns and the instability of commodity markets that frequently devastate efforts of the food-deficit nations to strengthen their economies and rural infrastructures. Again, it becomes a responsibility of the churches to help generate a commitment among the American people to cooperate in making international trade advantageous for the poorer nations which now struggle to overcome poverty and hunger.

Unfortunately, the early response of the U.S. government to these proposals has been at the level of only token support. But if that support grows, and if growing U.S. support is accompanied by the increasing support of other affluent nations—to the point that up to 10 percent of the world's military budget is rechanneled in this direction—the new World Food Council will move a long way toward helping the food-deficit nations take the steps outlined earlier in this chapter.

But we must recognize that the Council is calling for a quality of international responsibility and generosity that has not fared well among the affluent nations. Glimpses of it have been seen from time to time, but the world now needs more than glimpses. It needs sustained, generous caring. And such caring must manifest itself soon if a hunger-free world is to be built in the next two decades.

Ample evidence indicates that movement toward this future will not occur unless the reigning values of our time are dethroned. Other, more promising values must guide the way to a hunger-free future.

The Christian church knows the source of those values, and it must lose no time rediscovering them and helping the world put them into practice.

CHAPTER 4

God's Generosity and Our Responsibility

The Bible is a better source of insight about food and hunger than most Christians have realized. Nothing is more important for biblical religion—and for our world today—than what people do about daily bread. If now we recover the biblical perspectives upon food and let them shape our thought and actions, we shall become a church that is freshly alive to God's truth. And we shall find that this truth arms us for a surprisingly crucial role in a hungry world.

A clue to how important the subject of food was for biblical writers is the frequency with which it is mentioned. The word "bread" appears no less than 321 times and "eat" 420 times in the Revised Standard Version. To be sure, in some settings we find little or nothing instructive in the use of such words, but often what the Bible says about food reflects profound convictions that are central to its meaning for us today.

Look first at the Old Testament. The Creator placed Adam and Eve in a garden amply able to nourish them. He promised to deliver his people from bondage into a land "flowing with milk and honey." He works to lead the human family to an ultimate fulfillment where swords are transformed into plowshares and there is "a banquet of rich fare for all the peoples."

The same concern was continued and intensified in the early church. For instance, the only miracle account occurring in all four Gospels is Jesus' feeding of the multitude. Matthew reports Jesus' teaching that one test by which people will be judged is whether or not they have given food to the hungry and drink to the thirsty. And three Gospels attest that Jesus instituted a special sharing of bread and wine among his followers that, according to Paul, he wished to be continued "in remembrance of me."

Even a brief sampling of scriptural references to food suggests how rich and varied this theme is in the chief sourcebook of the church's faith. A helpful vantage point from which to analyze the Bible's message about food is the fourth petition of the Lord's Prayer: "Give us this day our daily bread." Jesus' prayer has been prized by generation after generation as an engaging digest of his teaching. The third-century theologian Tertullian aptly described the Lord's Prayer as "a brief form of the whole gospel," and the contemporary New Testament scholar Joachim Jeremias calls it "the clearest and . . . richest summary of Jesus' proclamation which we possess."[1]

When we seek the meaning of this portion of the Lord's Prayer in relation to the total biblical faith, we discover fresh horizons opened for our thinking and acting at four

41

principal points. It helps us understand (1) that God has created the entire universe in such a way that it can provide every person with the food necessary for a full life; (2) that hunger results from our disrupting the intended order of God's creation; (3) that God has acted in Jesus Christ to free the creation from the forces that keep the human family from responsibly using and sharing his gifts; and (4) that the church is called to spearhead the extension of Christ's liberating work to the whole creation in every age.

We shall now look closely at each of these four points and begin to learn their meaning for our mission in a hungry world.

(1) GOD'S GENEROSITY AS CREATOR AND EXEMPLAR

When Jesus taught his followers to pray, "Father . . . give us this day our daily bread," he was affirming Israel's faith that God always acts generously toward the creatures whom he has made dependent upon his good gifts. Every person experiences that generosity through God's provision of food for our bodies. The Genesis creation story proclaimed God's care for Adam, Eve, and every subsequent person: they were placed in a garden amid "trees pleasant to look at and good for food" (NEB). Despite human disobedience, God faithfully preserves the fruitfulness of the earth for our nourishment: "He veils the sky in clouds and prepares rain for the earth; he clothes the hills with grass and green plants for the use of man" (Ps. 147:8 NEB).

Israel knew that the only fitting response to such generosity is to give God thanks and praise, and to serve him by gladly doing his will. The Genesis story explains that this response is possible because humans are the only creatures made "in the image of God"—every person possesses the ability to know, enjoy, and serve God. This ability equips us for our awesome and distinctive human responsibility: a share in God's task of nurturing his creation toward the realization of its full potential. We are to "till and keep" the creation as God's stewards, exercising a "dominion" that is modeled upon his.

Responsible human dominion requires respectful, loving maintenance of the dynamic harmony and fruitfulness of God's creation. When we fulfill his will for the creation faithfully, we help it function properly and preserve its benefits for all. The creation cared for nourishes its inhabitants; the creation abused does not.

The Israelites and the early Christians alike knew that every person's responsibility to care for the creation in a God-like manner extends into the realm of human relationships. He gives us a nurturing responsibility for one another, and the Bible insists that the same radical generosity with which God cares for us is the standard that must guide human interaction. The Christian church knows that the definitive expression of God's generosity is the gift of his Son, and that his love for humanity went so far that he gave even his life. Each person is to be to others

43

like Christ, giving himself unreservedly so they may grow to the new life God intends for them.

Some Christians today tend to make an unbiblical separation between love and justice, claiming that one or the other must guide our response to the hungry world. This is unfortunate, because it obscures their inseparability in God's action and the consequent necessity of both directing responsible human action. God's stance toward us is one of loving, demanding nurture. He works to bring the whole human family—and each person—to the complete realization of the blessedness which is both his crowning gift to us and our fulfillment. That blessedness consists in becoming like him; because he is love, our blessedness consists in loving as he loves.

The purpose of our compassionate, demanding nurture of the human and nonhuman creation, therefore, is to ensure the presence of that dynamic harmony and fruitfulness (shalom) that helps people grow in their ability to love.

The Old Testament frankly admits that Israel often failed to nurture God's creation according to his intention. Because of this breakdown, poverty and hunger became the lot of some. But the Israelites repeatedly sought to restore an equitable share of God's bounty to the disadvantaged. Such action was viewed as both the duty of the community and the right of the needy. With a compassionate and just God as the exemplar of proper conduct, they could undertake nothing less.

Care of the needy was too important to be left to chance or to voluntary philanthropy. Successive legal codes sought to guarantee their protection. For instance, so that the poor would not remain permanently in debt, the law required that all debts be forgiven every seventh year (Deut. 15:1-2). The poor had the right to glean any food left behind after harvest, and owners were urged not to strip their fields, vineyards, or olive trees of all their produce (Deut. 24:19-21; Lev. 19:9-10). Every third year, owners were expected to give the poor a tithe of all crops grown (Deut. 14:28-29; 26:12).

Repeatedly prophets summoned Israel to repent of her failures and to perform the righteous deeds that God intends. Isaiah emphatically declared God's will: "Is it not to share your bread with the hungry and bring the homeless poor into your house?" These are no token acts; they are reflections of God's radical generosity. The person who performs such deeds will know the matchless joy of doing what he has been created to do, of sharing as God shares: "If you pour yourself out for the hungry and satisfy the desire of the afflicted, . . . you shall be like a watered garden, like a spring of water, whose waters fail not" (58:10-11).

The passing of the centuries has brought us a far vaster body of knowledge about human beings and the universe than either Israel or the early church possessed. But what they saw to be fundamentally true about human dependence and responsibility is no less true today. All persons—male and female, young and old, underfed and

45

overfed——have a common need and destiny. We are dependent for our sustenance and development upon natural forces with which we interact daily, as well as upon a network of human relationships to which we are tied inextricably. Today, as never before, humankind possesses the technological power to shape those forces and that network. Its possession presses urgent questions upon our time. How shall the created order be shaped? By whom and to what ends shall it be directed? Dare we continue to make it favor the privileged minority?

The biblical witness does not map a precise course for us, but it does provide an accurate compass. It reminds us that the natural and social environment in which we live is intended by the Creator to nurture every man, woman, and child toward fulfillment. Moreover, every person has the God-given responsibility to help direct this nurturing process as well as the God-given right to receive its benefits.

In a world painfully divided between the affluent and the poor, that responsibility and right are endangered on both sides of the dividing wall. Ironically, the danger will be met successfully only if the two groups discover their solidarity and move across the wall to aid each other. By doing so both will participate most responsibly in God's nurturing of his creation. Both also will thereby receive what they most need for the fulfillment of their humanity.

For the affluent this requires discovering new processes by which they can radically share themselves and their resources with the needy. They then will learn how much more blessed it is to give than to covet; by sharing generously they will do what they were created to do. Their radical sharing also will enable the poor to develop themselves sufficiently to exercise the right and responsibility which are essential if they are to realize their humanity. Without that act of solidarity, the impoverished millions will remain shackled by their struggle to survive. But once their hold upon life is made more secure, they have opportunity to rejoice in God's goodness and to extend it to others. This they can do by freely sharing their knowledge with the overprivileged millions that the truly rich life does not come through an accumulation of things and money. The choicest treasures come otherwise—through discerning the value of gifts that are ours already, especially the gifts of caring relationships with one another, with the earth, and with the Creator.

(2) HUMAN DISRUPTION OF CREATION

When we pray for daily bread, we express our dependence upon a God who gives food through a complex interplay of natural and social processes. We are asking him to uphold the orderliness of his creation so that it can bear its intended fruit for all. But our prayer is colored by what the Bible teaches regarding the ways that God's good creation is violated. In the Lord's Prayer we pray that God will provide nourishment in spite of the dark shadows cast by trespasses, temptation, and evil.

In teaching his followers to recognize the power of these forces, Jesus again affirms the outlook of Israel. The Genesis story shows that even though God made human beings the crown of creation, Adam and Eve desire more than they have been given. Consequently, they are vulnerable to the serpent's tempting appeal to reach beyond their limits for the forbidden fruit that will let them know good and evil like God. Seeking to have more so that they will become more, they grasp for more only to become less: "Because you have done this you are accursed more than all cattle and all wild creatures" (Gen. 3:14 NEB).

Israel and the church have found in the Genesis story a sobering truth about every person. Again and again we are tempted to overstep boundaries in pursuit of more than we need and can safely receive. But we cannot do so with impunity. When our greed yields to temptation, we disrupt the orderliness of God's creation and thereby sow seeds of misery. Because a moral order pervades human affairs, individuals and groups alike eventually reap what has been sown.

Repeatedly the prophets voiced God's judgment upon Israel's covetous ways. "Shame on those," said Micah, "who lie in bed planning evil and wicked deeds. . . . They covet land and take it by force; if they want a house they seize it" (2:1-2 NEB). The seriousness of such offenses was stated with telling force by Ben Sira in the Apocrypha: "The bread of the needy is the life of the poor; whoever deprives them of it is a man of blood. To take away a neighbor's living is to murder him; to deprive any employee of his wages is to shed blood" (Ecclus. 34:21-22).

Frank recognition that wealth often is a sign of greed and callousness was evident in Jesus' teachings. The exploitative accumulation of material goods is not compatible with the service of God: "No one can serve two masters. . . . You cannot serve God and mammon" (Matt. 6:24; Luke 16:13). Those who do make money their idol abdicate their responsibility to the Creator and disqualify themselves for his kingdom: "It is easier for a camel to go through the eye of a needle than for a rich man to enter the kingdom of God" (Mark 10:25).

Israel knew that so powerful are greed and callousness that they can make even the state an exploiter of the poor: "Shame on you!" cried Isaiah; "you who make unjust laws and publish burdensome decrees, depriving the poor of justice, robbing the weakest of my people of their rights, despoiling the widow and plundering the orphan" (10:1-2 NEB).

In the Old and New Testaments intimations are found that the disruption of God's good creation reaches even beyond the human realm. The world of nature, says Paul, exists in a "bondage to decay"; it too waits for deliverance (Rom. 8:21). Moreover, we must cope with powerful impersonal forces—what Paul called "the rulers of this age" (I Cor. 2:8)—which work to create moral blindness and thus to thwart God's design for the human family. Each generation faces updated forms of the serpent that lured Adam and Eve away from the life that God intended for them.

The Bible candidly admits the power of the assaults upon God's creation. Their cumulative effect across the years has resulted in stark poverty and debilitating hunger for millions today. When our prayer for daily bread takes the world's hungry masses into view, we can see how mammoth is the task of making God's generous purpose prevail. We also begin to see how appropriate it is that our prayer for bread is joined to the petitions that follow. For we who are part of the affluent world must ask God's forgiveness for the trespasses whereby we have contributed to the plight of the poor. We must ask that he lead us from the ever-lurking temptation to rank our whims above their needs, and that he deliver us from the evil forces seeking to make us forget that this is God's world and that he "is the ruler yet."

(3) CHRIST, THE BEGINNING OF THE NEW CREATION

Those whom Jesus taught to pray "Thy kingdom come, thy will be done on earth as it is in heaven," shared Israel's yearning for the blessedness that God intends for his creation. Eventually he will bring "new heavens and a new earth," a kingdom in which God's shalom is actualized and his goodness is enjoyed by all its citizens.

The New Testament reflects the early church's growing awareness that God's new beginning for his creation had dawned in the life of Jesus of Nazareth; he was the long awaited Messiah sent by God to inaugurate the kingdom. In his deeds people saw the outpouring of God's creative love. Life's joys were given to those who had been deprived of them: the blind received sight, the hungry were fed, the sick healed, the sinful forgiven. The true order of God's creation had broken into history with such visibility that now the human family could know what the Creator intends for them. So closely did Jesus seem linked to God's purpose for his creation that some affirmed that he had played a role in the universe's origin: "In the beginning was the Word," said the Fourth Evangelist; "all things were made through him. . . . And the Word became flesh and dwelt among us."

The early church knew that Jesus was a man who, more than any other, exemplified the responsible life that God intends for every person. As a man, Jesus experienced the pressures that push all toward conformity to the conventional wisdom of the world. The "rulers" of the age had shown him how well he would fare were he to seek his own advancement. But Jesus refused to yield to the temptation to grasp for more; he gave himself unswervingly to the service of God and others, even when it became clear that this course would result in a cruel death.

Good Friday is the sign of the costly victory that he won over the rulers of the age, and his Easter resurrection confirmed that a new beginning had dawned for the whole world. To the persons who attempt to live as he lived, to love with the same radically responsible love, his

Spirit is given to sustain them in their struggle and to allow them anticipatory tastes of the joys of his kingdom. Such persons constitute the church, whose mission is so to embody the pioneering ways of Jesus that it becomes a sign of God's intention for his creation and a basis for hope that eventually God's will shall be done throughout the earth.

How did Jesus respond to the hungry people of his day? On occasion he miraculously fed multitudes to show the quality of God's dawning kingdom, but we must ask why Jesus and his disciples did not spend more of their time directly feeding the hungry. The reason is suggested by Jesus' reply to the tempter's proposal that he assuage his hunger and prove his prowess by turning stones into bread. Jesus refused, saying, "Man shall not live by bread alone, but by every word that proceeds from the mouth of God" (Matt. 4:4). Here Jesus acted consistently with what we have seen of the Old Testament's appreciation of the social and natural processes through which people receive the Creator's bounty—processes which when shaped according to God's will are productive of bread and his other gifts as well. Similarly, Jesus taught his disciples (Matt. 6:25-33) not to be anxious about their food and clothing. Instead they should seek first God's kingdom, for when God's will for the creation is obeyed, it will provide all gifts essential for life. Jesus was not claiming that food is unimportant; he was affirming that God's way of giving it is through the right ordering of individual and corporate life, including those agricultural and societal processes by which food is produced and distributed.

The early church knew that the kingdom had not yet come in such fashion as to sweep away all that resists God and his intention for the creation. Even in the church there was abundant evidence that sin continued. But Christians persisted in the conviction that the day of perfect fulfillment will come and that history now moves under God's quiet governance toward its destination. Then God's children shall "serve him day and night. . . . They shall hunger no more, neither thirst any more; . . . and God will wipe away every tear from their eyes" (Rev. 7:15, 16, 17).

(4) GOD'S NEW CREATION AND THE CHURCH

When we pray, "Give us this day our daily bread," we do so knowing that for the complete fulfillment of this and our other petitions we must await that day known only to God when his will is perfectly done within the entire human family. But our waiting is an active waiting, for we who pray the Lord's Prayer place ourselves at the Lord's service, and we discover that he summons us to seek that for which he has taught us to pray.

We are sent on a pioneering mission to make known God's good purpose for the entire creation and to help implement that purpose in ever-widening realms of life.

What is especially striking about the first-century church's manner of embarking upon that mission is the emergence of a new style of caring for one another that anticipated the life of the kingdom whose cataclysmic arrival they thought to be imminent. In Acts 2 and 4 we learn that the first Christians in Jerusalem shared their goods with one another as need arose. In Paul's writings we catch glimpses of the collection he organized among the Gentile churches on behalf of needy Christians in Jerusalem (I Cor. 16:4; II Cor. 8:9). In Acts 6 we discover that a central initial task of the Apostles was to wait on tables, serving those who gathered to share the community's meals. We know too that from the earliest years Christians continued to share bread and wine as they had been commanded by Jesus. Here was a constant sign of their solidarity with him and with one another, as well as a foreshadowing of the great banquet that the human family ultimately will share in God's kingdom.

From the first century to the twentieth, the church has attempted to fulfill its mission in ways that address existing needs and opportunities, as well as in ways that reflect its current understanding of the gospel and the world. Today a careful study of our hungry world and of our faith compels the church to take vigorous action in four closely related realms. For the moment they will be stated in summary form. Later chapters will examine them more closely.

First, the church's perception of God's intention for his creation must be sharpened by fresh and probing study of the sources of Christian wisdom. Too long the church has allowed its preoccupation with otherworldly and individual salvation to result in neglect of its responsibility for the entire world's redemption. And too often what the church has thought to be a properly Christian stance toward the world has been shaped more by secular values and assumptions than by the gospel. Our mission to extend Christ's redemptive work to the whole created order requires that we expend the effort necessary to understand what light the church's theological and ethical resources cast upon the establishment of a new global society organized so as to provide the food and other essential gifts that God intends for all.

Second, the church must make its vision of God's new creation the basis for reshaping its own corporate life so that it better exemplifies the radically caring relationships that God intends for all. The food crisis challenges the church to put the gospel into practice. It must candidly ask how its own habitual ways of thinking and acting perpetuate the secular patterns that impoverish some and satiate others. The church also must move beyond its own walls to help correct the food and justice deficits that plague the human family. This it should do by generously using its resources to initiate processes that demonstrate how the natural and social environments in every land can become productive of the food that God intends for all. And until the food-producing and food-distributing systems of every nation are able adequately to overcome hunger, the church must help provide hungry people with their daily bread.

Third, the church must encourage individuals and

families to discover new, more appropriate lifestyles that end waste and help the poor receive their just share of the earth's resources. As the church fosters this embodiment of Jesus' way, it will move directly counter to powerful social pressures that urge the affluent to consume more and more. The church then will become a rallying point for greed-resisters committed to the search for more responsible ways of thinking and acting.

Fourth, the church must undertake a probing critique of secular social patterns that deny adequate nutrition to multitudes. We must not hesitate to voice God's judgment upon economic and governmental systems that perpetuate covetous and unjust ways. Whatever institution, ideology, or policy promotes or tolerates an insufficient food base for any person must be exposed as offensive to God and unworthy of humankind. And lest her critical voice become another shrill sound in our society, the church must work constructively with those who shape public thought and policy to find ways for the fruits of God's good earth to be produced responsibly and shared equitably with all.

PART 2

Deeds Required
for a Time of Crisis

Our knowledge about the world hunger crisis must now be put to good use. The chapters that constitute Part 2 of this book are intended to help the church discover deeds that are genuinely capable of moving our hungry world to a better future. These chapters reflect on the objectives of Christian action in four realms and offer examples of how some Christians already are working to realize objectives.

The first chapter briefly establishes a basis for comprehensive, step-by-step action; then the four following ones examine the church's responsibility for heightening awareness, mobilizing resources, developing responsible lifestyles, and reordering public priorities.

CHAPTER 5

Setting Our Sights

In the preceding chapter we saw that the church's fundamental mission is to continue Jesus' work of pioneering the responsible life that God intends for all people. It labors to make his ways known and accepted in an expanding circle of human relationships. As God's will is done in our hungry world more nearly as it is in heaven, the people who now are deprived of bread and justice increasingly will receive the good gifts that he desires for the human family; and those who wittingly or unwittingly have caused deprivation also will discover the way opened to a better life.

Growing numbers of denominations and congregations have begun to explore the meaning of human responsibility for this era of global hunger. Some observers predict that this interest will be a fad of short duration. They suspect that when Christians in our privileged nation recognize the extent to which familiar American ways are challenged by the masses' demand for food and justice, their concern for the hungry will result in merely token aid which makes little dent upon the problem.

The skeptics may be proven right, for the great

temptation of the American church is to talk much about hunger but to provide only surface remedies that make little demand upon us. On the other hand, it is possible that the skeptics are in for a surprise—this crisis may well shake the churches into new life. Such a possibility is encouraged by the fact that Christians in the United States and other affluent nations are discovering that the hunger crisis is also a crisis for us. Through it God judges us for our unthinking complicity in the perpetuation of humankind's misery, and he summons us to put the gospel into practice by working unreservedly to build a hunger-free world. As American Christians heed this summons in league with brother and sister Christians around the world, the ecumenical church can become a potent catalyst for change, for it is more widely dispersed and more deeply rooted than is any other global institution. The universal church is in a unique position to pioneer fresh patterns both among the hungry and among the affluent—as well as to help establish solidarity between the two groups. It is an auspicious moment for the church to rise to its role as the principal instrument through which God works to make his will known and obeyed throughout the earth.

We dare not attempt or expect too little.

A WAY TO PROCEED

For American Christians to play their proper part in this drama, they must move into action in four realms. Steps should be taken (1) to help affluent people recognize both the gravity of the hunger crisis and the way beyond it; (2) to mobilize church resources so that they work maximally for bread and justice; (3) to develop personal lifestyles that allow the affluent to end waste and combat greed; and (4) to make our political and economic institutions more effectively address the pain and causes of hunger.

So vast and complex is the hunger crisis that the church must be present in all four of these interrelated realms. What is learned by action in any one realm will enrich involvement and enhance impact in the other three. In each realm congregations and other groups will find action steps that are elementary and that can be taken with relative ease. As the beginning step is taken, the group must be watchful for additional steps that bring deeper, more demanding involvement.

The following diagram will help in planning a program of disciplined church response that is both comprehensive in scope and intensive in penetration.

Increasing scope of response

	Heightening awareness	Mobilizing church resources	Developing responsible lifestyles	Reordering public priorities
Step 1 - A Beginning				
Step 2 - A Little More				
Step 3 - Still More				
Step 4 - Much More				

Increasing intensity of response

Movement through the categories of the grid is both horizontal (developing action in all four realms) and vertical (developing ever more intensive action in each realm). For each of the four realms there are appropriate elementary steps by which a beginning can be made, then additional steps—"a little more," "still more," and "much more"—which mark progress toward deeper, more effectual levels of action.

When this approach has been used by Christian groups to help plan a disciplined, comprehensive response to world hunger, it has been found very useful. Those who wish now to employ it as their own tool must decide exactly how they will plan and implement their action. They must determine which concrete deed or deeds will fill each box of their grid. Decisions about responsibility for follow-up must be made clear to all.

Because people have different gifts and opportunities, the action that is "a beginning" for one group in the realm of mobilizing resources, for example, may be "still more" for another. Each group should begin where its interest is strongest and the likelihood of progress appears greatest. John Wesley's observation is helpful: "When we act on the light that has been given to us, more light will be given." Whatever route a group takes on the basis of the "light" it receives, it should aim to develop appropriate deeds for every category of the grid. For we all have been summoned to become involved comprehensively and intensively in the struggle to end hunger and injustice.

CHAPTER 6

Heightening Awareness

When Americans learn about hungry people in a land such as Bangladesh, they characteristically are tempted to make a small contribution to a relief organization, then to return to their routines with the comfortable feeling that they have done their part to combat hunger. Today many Christians are settling for this response to the hunger crisis (as data in the following chapter will detail), but fortunately some are recognizing the utter inadequacy of so minimal a response. This is tokenism—the gesture of offering too little for the solution of problems that require much more. Token aid does not feed many people; nor does it go far toward correcting the injustices that produce hunger. And it has the regrettable effect of confirming givers in their convenient blindness to their own involvement in the causes of hunger.

A fundamental task of the church is to help people overcome this blindness by fitting them with new lenses for seeing themselves and the world. Only such clear-sightedness will move us to the sanity and generosity with which we must fulfill our responsibility as caring human beings. Much has been given to us, and much is now required of us.

Part 1 of this book has explored what will be seen when one takes a clear-sighted look at the hunger crisis. Such sociological, historical, and theological analysis provides the necessary knowledge base for shaping deeds that are capable of ending hunger. But before we can go far toward doing such deeds, we need to understand and cope with the fact that our society has conditioned us to respond in a minimalist way to the hunger crisis. We must confront the internal and external pressures that restrict Americans' generosity and make tokenism an alluring alternative.

THE POWER OF TOKENISM

Our American society, like every other society, provides its members with a set of standardized mental "lenses" through which to view and interpret their experience. Like the lenses in eyeglasses, they help us to see other things but are not themselves easily seen by us. These mental lenses subtly condition what we are able to see and how we respond to what we see. Because they vary little among most persons in the same society, they tend to establish a common way of thinking, valuing, feeling, and acting that is prized as the key to group and individual identity.

Some nonconforming Americans have refused to accept the lenses prescribed by our society, and in some sectors of our life a single mode of thought and action is not expected. Nevertheless, we can spot certain recurring mental and behavioral patterns that are basic to "the American way of life" and that particularly mark the persons who have been closest to the mainstream of our national life. One of the most dominant of these patterns is evident in the success story that countless Americans tell about themselves or hope soon to be able to tell. The variations on it are numerous, but its kernel is familiar: "I have worked hard to get ahead and to earn as much money as I can. I want a good life for myself and my family, so I shall buy whatever my money entitles me to. Some people didn't make it as well as I did, but since they had basically the same opportunity I had, they got no more and no less than they deserved. They will have to lift themselves up by their own bootstraps. If they try to take what belongs to me, I shall fight them. But to those who need help badly, I'll be charitable and make a little gift."

The assumptions, attitudes, and values that underlie this statement have enjoyed a long history in this country. They helped energize our young nation's remarkable conquest of a vast land possessing seemingly endless natural resources. The Frenchman Alexis de Toqueville, observing this westward expansion early in the nineteenth century, wrote that "here is a civilized people who are also the most grasping nation on the globe." Through the nineteenth and twentieth centuries the American people found much to grasp for and did it with phenomenal success, and today we possess unprecedented material abundance. So visible and attractive has been this national success that many Americans continue to feel compelled to duplicate it in their own lives, and some in other nations seek the road to similar success.

Direction for the pursuit of national and individual prosperity has come chiefly from our economic ideology and institutions. As Secretary of the Treasury Simon remarked in 1975, the free enterprise system is "the rock upon which we have built our earthly kingdom." The hard inner core of that rock is the drive to maximize profit and to raise our standard of living. For industry this requires producing and selling more and more. For consumers it requires purchasing and desiring more and more. In the name of "the good life," our economic system adroitly nourishes the greed of producer and consumer alike, and it devours increasing amounts of the earth's non-renewable resources.

We must not overlook the fact that some individuals and corporations that have benefited from the system have made generous contributions to charitable causes. But typical Americans' charity is entirely disproportionate to the need of those helped. This should not be surprising, for our economic system's overwhelming interest is in providing more for those who already have gained from it, not in providing for others or for the good of the whole society. Economist John Kenneth Galbraith has remarked perceptively that "we are led, as a nation, . . . to adopt numerous of the least elegant postures of wealth. Though we have much, and much of the remainder of the world is poor, we are single-mindedly devoted to getting more. . . .

We do, each year, provide some aid for others. But first we have a prayerful discussion of whether or not we can afford the sacrifice."[1]

Essentially the same stance determines the United States' relationship to the hungry nations. A later chapter will consider this issue in some detail. For now we shall note only that Americans tend to view these nations with a mixture of contempt and pity. Since they have not achieved the prosperity we have, we are inclined to suspect that they are inept or otherwise undeserving. With our chief responsibility perceived as the maximization of our own strength, we assign little importance to the task of aiding the development of Third World nations. Such aid that we do give constitutes a small fraction of our surplus wealth (in 1975 it was 1/5 of 1 percent of our Gross National Product), and in recent years it has been sent primarily to those nations that we believe can be most useful to us economically and militarily.

Today growing numbers of Americans are discovering that serious flaws exist in our earthly kingdom and in the rock upon which it rests. An abundance of material goods does not satisfy our deeper longings; divorce, crime, unemployment, and suicide rates soar; protests mount from the privileged and the neglected alike. We sense that our great military might does not provide security in today's world; in fact, heavier and heavier spending for armaments may well be heightening our insecurity. A telling symbol of our condition is the affluent's difficulty with food: overeating is a major factor accounting for heart disease, the nation's chief health problem.

God's creation will not tolerate unlimited abuse. Today it is striking back, and we are reaping what we have sown. Because the victims of our excess are crying out too loudly to be ignored, history appears to have brought us to a pregnant moment when thoughtful Americans are aware that our way of life needs scrutiny and overhaul.

TOWARD A NEW WAY OF SEEING

The time has come for the church to challenge the underlying convictions and values that have led our nation to embark upon a course that is suicidal for itself and dangerous for the rest of the world. The church will be able to do so constructively only if it is clear about its alternative vision of human responsibility in God's world. To possess that vision the church must resolutely set aside the lenses provided by American society and look at the hungry world through the lenses provided by biblical faith. It then will make three important discoveries.

The first discovery will be that Americans—Christians and non-Christians alike—have been captive to the "rulers of this age" and to sin. We have surrendered control of our thoughts and actions to the norms of an acquisitive, exploitative society. We can afford ever more material goods and armaments but not decent health, nutrition, and education for deprived millions. The reigning norms tell us that we have acted properly—according to economic "laws," "national security," and our "rights"—but the biblical faith exposes our deeds as an abdication of elementary human responsibility. The power of present-day rulers has been most evident in our society's ability to nourish greed and make us ignore the fact that our excessive consumption has been at the expense of other persons' necessities, our own physical and mental health, and the earth's diminishing resources. As economist John Maynard Keynes noted in 1930, our system of accumulating wealth flourishes upon the pretense that "fair is foul and foul is fair": it discourages compassion and trust while rewarding greed and callousness.

Not only have the churches usually not objected to this moral blindness: by our behavior as institutions we have solemnly sanctioned many of its grossest misperceptions (e.g., competition is the "law of life"), and we have thankfully received our portion of the wealth amassed by the free enterprise system.

The sin of greed and callousness has a firm hold upon affluent Christians, and we are a basic cause of the world hunger crisis. The beginning of real wisdom is to admit that we are under God's judgment. The Christian gospel frees us for such cleansing confession by its affirmation that God forgives sin and empowers repentant men and women to make a fresh start. There is no place for paralyzing guilt and self-condemnation. We can embark upon the search for a more responsible social order in the confidence that we move in accord with God's renewing Spirit and the moral grain of history. What we sow in repentance and compassion will be reaped in bread and justice.

The second discovery will be that affluent Christians have been too remote from our hungry brothers and sisters. In spite of the publicity given the hunger crisis in recent years, there is still much that we do not know about the poor abroad and in our own communities. We suffer from a knowledge deficit in both the heart and the mind. Rarely do most of us come physically close enough to poverty to know poor persons by name and to sense their pain and despair. Until we do, we shall not be able to love them with a Christ-like love, and we shall not be moved to make their need our agenda. Nor have most Christians probed the underlying causes of hunger sufficiently to understand what we must do to stimulate the changes necessary to build a hunger-free world. We must undertake study inspired by commitment in order to make informed decisions about where our money, time, and skills shall be invested on behalf of a better future for all.

The third discovery will be that the churches have not yet adequately formulated a compelling and comprehensive vision of a new global society where food and justice are assured for all. Without that vision to guide us, we are hampered in our struggle against the prevailing mind-set of our time—a mind-set which is compounded of such lingering ideas as relativism and the survival of the fittest, and which lulls multitudes into complacent acceptance of poverty and injustice. "We are suffering from a metaphysical disease," writes British economist E. F. Schumacher, "and the cure must therefore be metaphysical."[2]

Pieces of the vision which can provide that cure have begun to emerge. The time is ripe for a long-range, ecumenical dialogue between practitioners and theorists from many realms who will put the pieces together so that all can more clearly perceive the contours of a global society that better embodies God's design for his creation. Such vision can help give depth to the World Food Council's outline of a hunger-free world and endurance to the persons who will be in the thick of the battle for such a world. This enormously important task cries out for the church's intellectual leaders. But the task is too important to be left to the experts alone. Every concerned Christian has a stake in its progress, and every congregation has wisdom to contribute to the dialogue.

CHAPTER 7

Mobilizing Church Resources

Some observers claim that world hunger has attracted a more vigorous response from churches than any cause since the civil rights movement in the 1960s. Whatever our measurement of the present response, the critical question is whether American Christians will make a serious, long-term commitment to battle the powerful forces that perpetuate hunger.

We must not underestimate the resources that the American churches potentially can marshal for this battle. In their membership of some 120 million persons is an enormous reservoir of compassion and skill. Numerous church-related institutions are engaged already in crucial tasks of education, health, and community development. Many programs in these realms (plus some in agricultural research and production) extend into Asia, Africa, and Latin America where they are implemented collaboratively with personnel from indigenous churches. Religious organizations receive 43 percent of Americans' philanthropic dollars. In 1974, the last year for which statistics are available, members of 44 Protestant denominations gave $1 billion for benevolent causes.

If the churches' resources are placed aggressively and persistently in the struggle for a hunger-free world, there is no doubt that they can make a contribution of historic consequence.

In this chapter we shall look closely at some of the significant steps already begun to enlist people and money in this cause. The experiences reported are signs of what can happen when Christians take their pioneering responsibility to heart. Other groups may well find them suggestive of steps they can take to mobilize their own resources.

ACTION IN THREE AMERICAN COMMUNITIES

The first of the three local ventures we shall consider has emerged in the small town of Blackshear, Georgia. Its 3,000 citizens have been awakened to the world food crisis through the activities of the 170-member Blackshear Presbyterian Church. This congregation is one of many participating in a denomination-wide program initiated in 1969 by the Presbyterian Church in the United States. The Blackshear congregation's pastor, the Reverend Richard Bass, is also the person chosen by his denomination's Hunger Task Force to catalyze and coordinate Presbyterian hunger-related programs throughout Georgia.

Sustained by his conviction that "we are all part of one global community where isolationism is unthinkable," Bass has worked methodically to help his congregation recognize the practical consequences of global solidarity. In October 1973 the hunger program in Blackshear began quietly with the appointment of a seven-member Hunger Task Force. These persons actively studied hunger issues for five months before attempting to bring them to the congregation's attention. A major focus of the initial study was the food needs of poor people in their own county, for Task Force members recognized their responsibility for hungry people close at hand, and they knew that involvement with hunger nearby would help them understand hunger far away.

In February 1974, with a sound knowledge base established, the Task Force began to plan how it would generate interest within the whole congregation. The decision was made to present the hunger issue for several minutes during each Sunday service in March. At one of these services worshipers were asked to count the number of times they took a breath in one minute, to realize that approximately that many people die every minute from hunger-related causes, and to reflect on their responsibility for the victims of hunger. The Task Force also prepared information about possible corporate responses to hunger and shared it with the congregation.

That was the beginning. Each succeeding autumn the Hunger Task Force was reconstituted in order to spread leadership opportunities to as many persons as possible.

Only eighteen months after the Blackshear church's hunger program began, one member made this assessment of what was happening: "First we had to be coaxed a little to help. Now we volunteer. That's how much our attitude has changed." Changed attitudes can best be seen in the variety and number of projects Blackshear Presbyterians have undertaken on behalf of the hungry.

1. Church leaders have spread information about the hunger crisis through newspaper articles, radio announcements, and personal presentations to local service organizations. Presbyterian youth have played "Baldicer" (a hunger simulation game) at church and have initiated its use in the local high school. The school also has been prompted by Presbyterians to become more aware of developing nations' struggle for a new global economic order.

2. The governing body of the congregation designated the offering received the first Sunday of each month for use in the fight against hunger. Record-size special offerings have been received for this cause on Easter Sunday. Teen-agers have raised money through "hunger walks"—each walker asking sponsors to pay a specified amount for every mile walked. This youth effort (along with others undertaken by Blackshear Presbyterians) has been carried out jointly with friends in the local United Methodist congregation. Most of the money raised for overseas relief and development has been channeled to ecumenically sponsored projects through Church World Service.

3. Families have been asked carefully to determine how far they can go in sharing their financial resources to help

75

overcome hunger. A "personal commitment" form was prepared that allowed each person to indicate what his or her course of action would be on behalf of the hungry. Each person's form was returned as part of the Easter offering. One family decided to give one-tenth of its grocery money to organizations fighting hunger. Another gives 3 percent of its total income to such organizations (in addition to its regular tithe given to the church). Some give an amount equal to what was spent for new Easter clothes. Some fast on specific days and give the money saved. Some give money as memorials to church members who have died. Some couples give in celebration of wedding anniversaries.

4. Church members worked with county officials first to initiate and then to help conduct a volunteer program disseminating information about food stamps and proper nutrition to needy people in the area. Church members once a week collect unsold food contributed by a local grocery store and distribute it to persons who cannot afford to buy it. And they write state and national political leaders to urge support of specific legislative proposals intended to combat hunger.

For the great majority of Christians the congregation continues to provide the principal opportunity for their affirmation of faith and their discovery of faith's meaning for life. But other patterns for Christians' corporate worship and nurture are emerging. One of the most striking is the clustering of individuals and families who choose to live in close community, developing patterns of simplicity and interdependence that deliberately challenge the reigning values of our society. It is a pattern which has recurred in varying forms throughout Christian history and which may well have fresh import for our time.

Mr. and Mrs. Richard K. Taylor and their two children joined such a community in Philadelphia several years ago. Taylor explains that the eighty people comprising the community lived in a dozen houses and supported a nonviolent training center. Their hope has been to find shared ways of implementing "Jesus' insights about not grasping for money." Taylor chose to earn an income of less than one-half his former earnings. Living expenses were cut through such measures as developing a community garden and a food cooperative, splitting up house costs among the ten persons who shared the same dwelling, making their own clothing and furniture or buying it at inexpensive shops, and relying on mechanically talented community members for repairs.

On the basis of his experience Taylor affirms that

it is important to try to begin to live in a way that, if widely adopted, would help reduce the negative impact of the economy on the ecosystem and on the poorer nations. Just as important is our discovery that our simple, cooperative way of life frees us in ways that were impossible in the past. Men and women are freed to share equally in household tasks, so that no one is unduly burdened with cooking, child care, or cleaning. Both women and men pursue a variety of educational, vocational, and social-change interests outside the home. No longer are we tied to the tyranny of nine-to-five jobs, taken only because of the income they produce. Most of us find that we can survive very well on part-time jobs. . . . We find all kinds of ways to enjoy one another and the world, whether through songfests, shared work, study groups, common worship, or recreation.[1]

The final local effort that we shall note is a collaborative project serving inner-city families in Cincinnati, Ohio. Ten churches banded together in January 1975 to form the "5-C Co-op"—that name a shortened form of the "Cincinnati Concerned Churches' Consumer Co-operative." The objective of the organization is to provide nutritious food at low prices for the elderly, the unemployed, and others with meager income.

The 5-C Co-op was initiated and is managed by the Reverend John Collins, a United Methodist minister who serves as District Program Assistant for his denomination's Cincinnati District. Each week two days of Collins' time are donated by the District to allow him to work with volunteers who assist in the purchase and distribution of food.

In each church an expediter receives grocery orders and advance payments, which then are passed on to Collins. Once a week he buys the food that will be needed from a wholesaler. Volunteers divide it and place it in two- and three-dollar sacks. Consumers who want meat pay an additional amount for it. Each church collects its weekly order, and co-op members then go to the church to collect what they have ordered.

Collins and his colleagues estimate that their cost-cutting methods save co-op members about 25 percent of the amount charged by supermarkets. Moreover the food they receive is fresh, and it has been carefully chosen for its nutritional value. Co-op leaders believe that this effort offers members another important value: "That benefit is one of social gratification—the feeling of contributing to the common good, of helping persons help themselves, and the sense of participating in a worthy neighborhood effort."

CHURCH WORLD SERVICE AND CROP

The major interchurch agency in the United States working to establish a hunger-free world is Church World Service. Since its establishment in 1946, this organization has sent some 5 billion pounds of food, clothing, and health supplies—valued at more than half a billion dollars—to needy people. Thirty denominations presently support CWS, which operates as a unit within the National Council of Churches. Its total program in 1974 was carried out at a cost of $33 million. Only 7 percent of each dollar that CWS receives is spent for administration and promotion.

In 1974 CWS distributed approximately 1,000 tons of food, and in 1975 it was anticipated that the figure would be at least double that. In disaster and emergency situations (such as after a severe hurricane) food distribution is made directly to victims, often at feeding centers. In its regular programs among the chronically poor, food is distributed in three ways: in health clinics and family service centers for nutritional supplementation and education, and as an incentive for introducing mothers and fathers to family planning; in "food-for-work" projects which engage men and women in agricultural and community development tasks, then pay for their services with food; and in institutional feeding for young children, for the elderly, and for the sick.

A major area to which Church World Service responded in the mid-1970s was the drought-stricken lands of Africa. In Niger and Ethiopia, for example, it provided high-protein foods for the malnourished; medicines for the sick; seedlings and seeds to replenish forests and revive pastures; tools and equipment for well-digging; vehicles to transport goods; and an innovative method of placing ladybugs in date palms to feed on the parasites infesting the trees, which supply one of Niger's most important cash crops. CWS also sent agronomists, nutritionists, and medical specialists—the two latter groups working chiefly among young children, nursing mothers, and the aged.

While CWS continues to be deeply involved in emergency aid to disaster victims, it has increasingly sought ways to provide long-range developmental aid that addresses the causes of poverty and hunger. A key feature of Church World Service's work is also its collaboration with national Christian councils in the more than forty developing nations where its assistance is offered. An international team, including indigenous leaders in each case, serves with approximately fifty North Americans to form an administrative and technical staff. CWS programs are also closely coordinated with those sponsored by the World Council of Churches.

A sometimes controversial facet of CWS policy has been its cooperation with the U.S. government's Food for Peace program. This program has donated U.S. foodstuffs to foreign lands and has allowed them to be distributed through CWS and other voluntary agencies. The amount of Food for Peace aid handled by CWS was severely reduced in 1975 because of government cutbacks, but during the preceding year government-donated aid accounted for 88 percent of all the food shipped by the agency. Critics pointed out that because U.S. foreign policy considerations determined where much of their food aid was given (a high proportion to U.S.-supported governments in Indochina), CWS and other religious bodies cooperating with the government program had become tools of U.S. political objectives. Changes during 1975 in both CWS and Food for Peace policy appeared to blunt the criticism, but CWS officials recognized that an important issue in church-state relations had been raised.

A large portion of the money and goods received by Church World Service comes from CROP, the ecumenical agency it created to solicit aid from communities across the nation. Most of the gifts received by CROP go to CWS, but contributors are given the option of designating their gifts for other religious agencies such as Lutheran World

Relief and Catholic Relief Services, or for secular agencies such as CARE.

CROP has developed a variety of ways to educate the public about world hunger and to sensitize consciences. A typical leaflet, published in 1974, conveys this message:

How Much Do You Care?

Do you care, say, $5 worth? That will buy two tickets to the movies, or a pizza after the game. $5 will also buy 125 packets of vegetable seed, enough for a small village to plant a community garden . . .

Do you care $50 worth? $50 will buy the lady of the house a permanent wave and a new girdle. It will also buy enough beans to feed 20 workers and their families for a month while they build a much needed school.

$850 worth? That's a chunk. Enough to buy a 7 h.p. garden tractor to mow your yard. Enough to buy a windmill that might make the difference between life and death to a whole community of people in time of drought. And if you're thinking of putting in a swimming pool . . .

God knows we have it to give. It's up to us to care.

The five chief methods used by CROP for soliciting gifts are (1) hunger walks (such as we saw in Blackshear, Georgia); (2) fasts by persons who ask sponsors to pledge a specified amount for every hour that no food is eaten (usually 24 to 30 hours); (3) direct door-to-door solicitations; (4) special projects such as giving up meals and contributing their costs; (5) friendship farms, which represent some portion of farmers' produce or livestock given directly to CROP.

UNITED METHODIST COMMITTEE ON RELIEF

Most of the large American denominations are engaged in relief and development projects similar to those operated by Church World Service, and at times the denominational programs are performed cooperatively with those of CWS. One of the chief denominational agencies operating both through its own and through ecumenical channels is the United Methodist Committee on Relief. Like most similar church agencies, UMCOR's activities were greatly expanded during the mid-1970s. Income from United Methodist congregations rose from $2.5 million in 1971 to $4.3 million in 1973 and to $6.1 million in 1974. By November 1975 (when this book went to press) UMCOR officials were estimating a total figure for 1975 of $10 million.

One of the chief areas receiving UMCOR attention has been Bangladesh. Since 1970 a total of $3.2 million has been committed to relief and rehabilitation programs there. Much of that aid has gone for emergency relief to flood and war victims. "Now, however," say UMCOR leaders, "the people of Bangladesh need more than relief. A wide range of social and economic measures must be undertaken in the name of Christ so that we may support them in their struggle for self-development and human dignity." Like CWS, UMCOR works through indigenous organizations. For example, it helped the Christian Commission for Development in Bangladesh (CCDB) to bring 24,000 acres of land under irrigation, thereby making possible multiple cropping in a dry area where previously it had been possible to plant only one crop annually. Local farmers there are now being recruited and trained as extension workers. Farmers will form cooperatives and receive a development loan from the CCDB, which also will provide technical and managerial expertise. As many as 12,000 farmers plus their families and persons providing supportive services will benefit from this project (altogether about 100,000 people). When farmers have repaid their development loans, the same funds will be used to launch similar ventures in other areas.

UMCOR support of medical programs in Bangladesh is coordinated through the office of the Christian Health Care Project of the National Council of Churches in Bangladesh. The Project emphasizes integration of family planning services with maternal and child care. This it does in the knowledge that a high infant mortality rate presses parents to have large families and that improved maternal and child health care facilitates the limiting of family size. The Project provides its family planning and health care services through the highly regarded Christian hospitals and dispensaries scattered throughout the country.

BY WAY OF CONSTRUCTIVE ASSESSMENT

We now must attempt some evaluation of the activities that have been surveyed in the preceding pages. Any

Christian committed to the struggle for a hunger-free world is grateful for the steady labors of pacesetters in communities such as Blackshear, Philadelphia, and Cincinnati, as well as for the work of persons who staff relief and development agencies in many lands.

Reflection upon these efforts and upon many others that the authors have observed prompts three clusters of comments about the direction of the churches' response to the world hunger crisis in the years ahead.

(1) Hungry people will not be fed and the conditions causing hunger will not be changed without extremely large sums of money. Although on first glance American Christians may appear to be giving large amounts to the fight against hunger, a closer look reveals that the level of giving is shockingly low. All the facts necessary to provide a definitive, updated picture of giving patterns are not available; we do not know, for example, how much the average person giving to UMCOR gives to other religious and secular agencies that are combatting hunger. Nevertheless, some figures that are available provide us a roughly adequate picture. It is not encouraging. For example, the average per capita amount contributed to all "benevolences" (hospitals, orphanages, missionary support, relief services, etc.) by 44 Protestant denominations in 1974 was nearly $24, about $2 monthly. This figure represented approximately ½ of 1 percent of the average American's income that year. The record amount anticipated by UMCOR for 1975 represents an average of only 9¢ a month from United Methodists.

Such figures are not surprising to persons familiar with the pattern of philanthropic giving in this country. After large amounts have been spent for ourselves, little is left for others. A 1972 study by the U.S. Department of Commerce revealed that Americans collectively spend five times the amount on "recreation" that they spend on "religion and welfare."

These data suggest how much remains to be done to overcome tokenism and lead American Christians to a more clear-sighted and generous response to the world's hungry millions.

(2) Funds that become available to the churches for their part in the fight against hunger must be allocated with careful attention to all the fronts on which the battle is to be waged. Our temptation is to give most of our help to those who are starving now. We dare not neglect such persons, but neither dare we slight the steps that must be taken now to prevent rapid escalation of hunger in the years ahead.

Consistent with the perspectives developed in this book we recommend allocation of available funds according to the following formula (the first three categories aimed chiefly for the food-deficit nations, and the last two for this country):

    (1) 20 percent for emergency relief and feeding programs;

    (2) 20 percent for agricultural and rural community development programs;

    (3) 20 percent to train agricultural and rural leaders;

(4) 20 percent to heighten the sensitivity of affluent Americans and facilitate development of responsible lifestyles;

(5) 20 percent to enable informed Christian witness in political and business arenas.

Constructive steps can be taken in each of these realms with a relatively modest increase of available funds. Accordingly, we suggest that, without cutting their current contributions to religious and humanitarian organizations, American Christians begin to give *an additional amount equaling 1 percent of their annual personal income* to organizations engaged in the battle for a hunger-free world. If we Christians make the psychological and economic changes that allow us to take this step, we may well discover that an even larger amount is more within our reach than we had supposed. We also will begin to look more critically and constructively at how we are spending the remaining 90-plus percent of our income. The way beyond tokenism then will have begun to unfold before us.

(3) Our cultural climate makes it extremely easy for American Christians to think that raising money is our major contribution to the battle against hunger. Other needs, however, must also be attended to if our responsibility is to be met. In at least six matters the quality of our intellectual and spiritual response to hunger is as crucial as the quantity of our funds. First, decisions about where money will be spent must be made in genuine collaboration with Third World colleagues (as well as with

representatives of deprived American minorities), so that we do not unwittingly impose a neo-colonialist pattern of donor rule and recipient dependency. Second, the chief purpose of the church's relief and development efforts is to formulate and demonstrate a standard of compassion and justice that can be adopted by the secular institutions whose proper work is relief and development.

Third, although the "task-force" approach can be a useful method of initially rallying individuals and groups to address the hunger problem, this approach can unwittingly foster tokenism by obscuring the necessity both for long-term commitment to the battle against hunger and for permanent changes in our accustomed patterns of individual and corporate action.

Fourth, we must be steadfast in the recognition that we shall make an enormous contribution to the eradication of hunger by seeking those changes in American life (and in ourselves) that will lead this nation to become a fully responsible partner in the world community. Fifth, we must recognize that the worship of the church is a fertile but too rarely tapped resource for teaching Christians the centrality of bread and justice in God's plan for the human family. "Give us this day our daily bread. . . . Do this in remembrance of me."

Finally, we must acknowledge that the church has a great deal to do to put its own house in order by ending the waste that characterizes many of our familiar ways— from the covered-dish supper to the preservation of separate denominations.

CHAPTER 8

Developing
Responsible Lifestyles

When concerned individuals discover the overwhelming magnitude of the world hunger crisis, they often are tempted to despair at the possibility of making any significant contribution toward its resolution. We must not yield to that temptation! Each of the chapters in Part 2 of this book proposes steps that are within reach of individuals as well as groups. Even more than in other chapters, the steps to be considered now are accessible to every American Christian. They help us to put our own inner houses in order.

A clean-up of our lifestyles is badly needed, for we casually waste food, energy, and other resources that are painfully scarce in most of the world. With our great buying power (recall the figures cited in chapter 1), we make purchases with little regard for their effect upon ourselves, upon others, and upon the earth. And increasing numbers of the industrial nations have followed our prodigal example.

Unless we care enough to stop this reckless consumption and waste, the hungry cannot possibly have just access to their portion of the world's resources, and we shall fully earn E. F. Schumacher's sharp judgment: "The world cannot afford the USA. Nor can it afford western Europe or Japan. In fact we might come to the conclusion that the earth cannot afford the 'modern world.' It requires too much and accomplishes too little. . . . The earth cannot afford, say, 15% of its inhabitants—the rich who are using all the marvelous achievements of science and technology—to indulge in a crude, materialistic way of life which ravages the earth." [1]

A critical part of the church's mission in a hungry world is to foster a recognition of the need for developing responsible lifestyles, to support persons who undertake such change, and to combat the skillful advertising techniques aimed at maintaining high levels of consumption and waste.

The church is no newcomer to the task of changing people's lives. The self-giving ways of Jesus' kingdom stood in sharp contrast to the self-seeking ways of the first-century world. Paul voiced a dominant theme of the early church when he exhorted Christians, "Do not be conformed to this world but be transformed by the renewal of your mind, that you may prove what is the will of God" (Rom. 12:2). Even in the early church not all Christians measured up to such a high standard. Compromise has recurred century after century, but the conviction has persisted that the daily lives of Christians must reflect the responsible, caring ways of Jesus. That conviction fortunately is being rekindled today, and growing numbers of Christians are committing themselves to the search for a simpler, less wasteful, and more responsible pattern of everyday living.

To help open up this path for more people, we shall look closely at the direction the gospel gives for lifestyle change, then at the differences that a more responsible lifestyle can make in today's world, and finally at how we can proceed to put such lifestyle change into effect.

DISCOVERING THAT THE GOOD LIFE IS THE RESPONSIBLE LIFE

The passage quoted from Paul's letter to the Romans emphasizes that personal transformation comes by way of a changed mind. Paul rightly saw that we act on the basis of what we think and feel is the good life. If our way of living is to change, our way of viewing life must first be changed. This is all the more true in a society that has great manipulative control through the mass media over the way we think and feel, and that does not hesitate to use its power to persuade us that the good life is the one that is most full of the latest creature comforts. Its message is the more we possess, the better our life. This is the most sinister myth of our time.

If the church is effectively to oppose this myth, we must hold the alternative vision for which we contend clearly in mind. We shall need to do considerably more than to clarify our vision, but that "more" will not be accomplished unless our vision is clear. On this issue the church is not impartial. The whole of the biblical witness points to the good life that God wants every person to enjoy. The church has affirmed through the centuries that its essence has been uniquely exemplified in Jesus of Nazareth. In him we find the embodiment of true, responsible humanity. He acts with the same compassion and generosity that characterize the Creator. He selflessly seeks the well-being of others. His needs are simple, and he quietly trusts that what is required for his sustenance will be provided without his greedily grasping for it. And he works to teach people the Creator's will, so that the processes of nature and society will bear their fruit for all.

The way of Jesus is the way of radical, creative sharing. We saw earlier that the biblical perspective upon sharing has no kinship with the tokenist mentality which leads many today to "share" their crumbs. The Bible, not Karl Marx, was the original proponent of the claim that whatever my neighbor needs for his personal fulfillment intended by God, that I must give as my means allow. Martin Luther incisively voiced the mainstream of Christian thought about responsible generosity with his insight that our refusal to share is *robbery of our neighbor*. He meant that what we "own" is held in trust for others; when we fail to share with those in need, we rob them of what God intends them to receive through us.

Gospel wisdom teaches us that responsible self-giving allows us to share both in the joy of Jesus' resurrection and in the pain of his crucifixion. The joy of new life does not come except by death of something of the old. To break with the standard patterns of our prodigal society will not be easy for us. Some will brand us as foolish and eccentric. Some will suspect us of undermining and betraying our nation. Some will view us as religious fanatics. We may find walls rising between ourselves and persons whose friendship we cherish. We may need to spend extra time and effort to find alternative, less wasteful ways of handling everyday chores. We may be forced into financial hardship by the decision that our present job contributes too much to the perpetuation of an irresponsible society and too little to the building of a responsible society. We may have to bear the burden of knowing that the consequences of our "foolishness" affect not just ourselves but persons close to us who do not share our commitment to lifestyle change. And we may need to resist pressures to have more children than we think is consistent with responsible parenthood and responsible world citizenship.

But if there is pain in the pursuit of responsible lifestyles, there is also satisfaction deeper than the pain.

CONSEQUENCES OF A RESPONSIBLE LIFESTYLE

The Christian life is a process of struggle toward total acceptance of Jesus' way as our own way. For affluent American Christians—as it was for the rich young ruler in Jesus' parable—there is no more difficult step in that struggle than coming to terms with our wealth. Jesus does not tell every American Christian what he told the rich young ruler, but he does confront every one of us with the necessity of finding the most responsible means of committing our total resources—time, money, skills—to the service of our needy brothers and sisters. Until we have responded to this demand, we are not free to hear what else Christ is summoning us to, nor are we free to receive what else he is offering us. And because the yes with which we answer his demand is also a no to the "rulers" which tempt us into the pitfalls of a wasteful society, our response frees us from the dissipation of our energies in the trivial diversions that compete for our time and dollars.

By heeding this demand and winning this freedom, we will not bring instant change to our communities. But our more complete identification with Christ and his way will teach us something new about his patience and hope. We shall learn to look patiently and hopefully for the places and occasions when we can help something of the life of his kingdom to break through and become operative in our society.

When we have learned that the good life is not a race for material abundance, we are ready for the discovery of riches that lie close at hand. Creative energies are released and blinders removed. We can take time to discover the vast treasures of nature. We can take time to discover depths of beauty in our spouses, our children, our parents, our friends, even our enemies. We can take time to read, to play, to think, to meditate, to pray, to laugh, to cry. We can take time to give more of ourselves to work on behalf of our disadvantaged brothers and sisters. And we can take time to share our discoveries with our overprivileged brothers and sisters.

When we have learned that simpler diets are sounder diets, a simpler life a sounder life, our health likely will improve. Potentially, more food and energy will be released for the hungry world. Food expert Lester R. Brown estimates that if Americans were to reduce their meat consumption by only 10 percent for one year, that act could free at least 12 million tons of grain for human consumption—an amount sufficient to feed 60 million people a year.

When we have established our independence from the acquisitive, exploitative ways of our society, we become convincing testimony to the fact that people do not have to live under their domination. We demonstrate that the sins of greed, waste, and exploitation are not inevitable. We are proof that redemption happens. Our example can not only encourage those who are similarly committed to pioneering responsible lifestyles, but it also may attract others to join in this pursuit of the good life.

As the search for creative, joyful "deprivation" spreads, it can become a force that must be reckoned with both by business and by government. They will see that a growing minority of Americans wants a standard of living lower as measured by dollar value but higher as measured by human value. Fortunately the automobile industry has recognized that many Americans no longer desire the large, gas-consuming, polluting cars that so long have symbolized our wasteful abundance. Some enlightened firms are seeking changes of corporate policy that will make them more responsive to human need. But what has been done by business and government so far is a small beginning. As more people become convinced that the good life is the responsible life, that small is beautiful, that enough is enough, they will need to carry their message into the arenas where government and corporate decisions are made. Hence, we must work politically to ensure that the reduction of our food consumption, for instance, leads to foreign policy developments that foster an increase of food production in the hungry nations.

Finally, our simpler lifestyles will allow us to move toward a sense of solidarity with the rest of the human family. We have long considered ourselves the greatest and strongest nation. In some respects we may be, but in other respects we clearly are not. Our personal lifestyles and national policies have put us out of touch with the outlook, the aspirations, and the achievements of most of humankind. We have much to gain by rediscovering the fact that we are primarily citizens of the earth and secondarily citizens of the United States.

GETTING STARTED

Fortunately we can learn from Christian men and women who already are at work developing viable expressions of the responsible life. In the remaining pages of this chapter we shall sit at their feet, learning what we can from their experience. Each reader should look for what can be assimilated and adapted to his or her own steps toward a more responsible lifestyle.

Roberta Neuman, from Placentia, California, points to nine realms in which her family is seeking a simpler lifestyle.

1. I plan a weekly menu so that almost all of the shopping can be done at one time. I also try to run all errands on the same day that I shop. Additional items (milk, bread, etc.) are secured by the use of a bicycle, or sometimes by foot-power.

2. We eat meat at the most 3 days a week. It takes more planning and an adventurous spirit with the cook book, but it makes meal preparation and consumption exciting. We're discovering that vegetables, cheeses, fish, fruit, eggs, etc. are not only nutritious, but they taste great, too. One added side-effect: we're losing weight that was unwanted while developing better eating habits.

3. We've taken out some of the decorative plants in our yard and put in a small garden with lettuce, asparagus, turnips, and zucchini. Even in suburbia, it's possible to find an area for growing your own food on a limited scale. It's a great family project, and the food tastes so much better.

4. Rabbit droppings plus worms equals fertilizer! It seems to do a reasonable job on the lawns, and it's a great way to use an otherwise unwanted by-product of our pet.

5. Car pooling didn't thrill Chuck because he wanted to be "free" to be late or early to work, but he tried it, found that there were advantages to discussing issues to and from the lab, and now he is an advocate of car pooling. He even uses his bike to go to the lab on weekends (7 miles), thus getting additional exercise as well.

6. I often form a car pool with neighbors or friends for weekly shopping or running errands. Friendships have

deepened because of this additional "unscheduled time" together.

7. We have long subscribed to the "old is beautiful" principle. In fact, we tend to drive our cars to death. Thanks to car pooling, biking, and public transportation (limited as it is), we will soon become a one-car family. It's possible, even with a busy "volunteer" schedule like ours.

8. Instead of buying a fan or air conditioner, we've put wind turbines on the house and are planting more trees. They have reduced the temperature by 8 to 10 degrees in the summer, and the house is bearable if not cool. Last winter our thermostat was set at 63. We wore sweaters, but found that it was a pleasant atmosphere for doing almost anything but sitting still for long periods of time.

9. We make use of our congregation's "things" closet of items that are needed occasionally but can be shared on a library-type basis—such items as a lawn mower, an edger, clippers, beds for unexpected house guests, camping equipment, kitchen mixers, and electric knives.

Mrs. Neuman adds that perhaps one of the greatest benefits to come from such steps is "the children's awareness as to what is 'necessary' in life and what are 'frills' that are nice but not really needed. . . . I've had a policy that any time I'm away from home for more than 5 days, I bring the children a gift. A year ago they suggested that toys are nice, but books, clothing, or even post cards or pictures about the places I go are better. They are more aware of the many people around the world who don't have even basic necessities while their friends continue to 'need' $35 skate boards, motorcycles, etc."

Some churches have begun to encourage members to consider appropriate lifestyle modification. A lengthy commitment form was developed recently by a group of United Methodist lay leaders and distributed widely. The "Covenant of Commitment" suggests a broad range of possible changes and encourages each group to revise and adapt the statement so that it fits their circumstances. Then the tailored statement becomes an authentic expression of what the group has agreed to do. They then can affirm: "This we will do together." A large portion of the Covenant deserves repeating here.

> We know from the scriptures that God commands his people to make the cause of the poor, the hungry, and the oppressed their own. If we are truly to practice our faith, then we cannot sit idly by while others suffer.
>
> Realizing that the response of many individuals can aid in the alleviation of world hunger, yet recognizing too that responses must be varied to meet individual circumstances, the following alternatives are offered as some of the ways in which you may personally join in this covenant of commitment.

Food Consumption
1. Choose one
    a. Abstain from eating meat three days per week.
    b. Cut meat consumption rate by 50 percent.
    c. Have one meatless meal per day.
2. Eliminate high sugar content foods from diet.
3. Serve smaller portions and encourage restaurants to do the same.
4. Replace some animal food intake with plant foods.
5. Be willing to accept and purchase different quality (grass-fed) meat.

6. Consider food produced by oppressed labor as "unclean."

Fuel and Energy

1. Maintain home and office temperatures no higher than 68 degrees.
2. Utilize public transportion or car pools for daily commuting.
3. Walk to areas within one mile of home when possible. (Work for building of sidewalks and bikeways.)
4. Consolidate shopping stops when driving and pool shopping trips with neighbors.
5. Utilize manufactured fertilizers for growing foods and fibers only.
6. Use natural fertilizers and pesticides on gardens and flowers.
7. Recycle resources with an emphasis on saving and using them wisely rather than wasting and discarding.
8. If purchasing a next car becomes necessary, buy a low-gas-consuming model.
9. Use less energy at home and office in lighting, air conditioning, etc.
10. Refrain from using known pollutants.

Simplified Lifestyle

1. Evaluate lifestyle. Change it to be more compatible with the environment and global responsibility.
2. Individuals commit an additional 2–5% of church pledges for use in hunger/energy/development programs.
3. Eliminate or restrict consumptive luxuries.
4. Emphasize hunger/energy/development themes in speeches and conversations.
5. Limit the family size to two children.
6. Encourage others that a simplified lifestyle can make a difference in changing the outlook of today's world.

7. Be open to the possibility that changing situations may make this pledge obsolete, but continue always to seek the best way to live for others.

Finally, we must note that some clusters of Christians have become so committed to helping stimulate personal lifestyle change that they now are preparing and distributing resources that can facilitate such change. One of the most enterprising is the group known simply as "Alternatives." Based in Greensboro, North Carolina, they produce a quarterly newsletter by the same name. They have authored *The Alternate Celebrations Catalogue* (an earlier version of which was the widely used *Alternate Christmas Catalogue*). This is an encyclopedia of provocative suggestions about how to celebrate birthdays, weddings, Thanksgiving, Christmas and other special events in simpler ways that "expand life for others."

The group's bookstore has gathered and distributes an array of books and pamphlets that treat different facets of the search for simpler lifestyles. Among the titles: *Clusters: Lifestyle Alternatives for Families and Single People; Diet for a Small Planet; Living Poor with Style; Creative Food Experiences for Children; A Manual of Death Education and Simple Burial; About Community Gardening; Organizing for Health Care;* and *Celebrations of Life.*

A CONCLUDING COUNSEL

As more and more American Christians recognize the need to reshape their personal lifestyles, they will discover that serious, persistent effort does not "just happen." Token change perhaps can come with relatively little effort, but it also vanishes quickly when pressures mount for a return to the familiar. The fact that our accustomed patterns have so firm a grip upon us prompts several concluding reflections about lifestyle change.

First, no one should expect to make far-reaching lifestyle change all at once. Athletes who are conditioning their bodies for a grueling sport know the importance of step-by-step preparation. Select your starting point, then gradually build upon it.

Second, do not underestimate the importance of personal clarity about why this change is being undertaken. To endure, the effort must be deeply rooted in the rich soil of the gospel—the gospel reflected upon again and again.

Third, recognize the importance of a supportive community. Members of one's family and other families in the congregation should talk openly about their struggle toward a responsible lifestyle. Each person needs the encouragement of brothers and sisters in Christ. Each needs to be reminded that Christ wants us to be joyously responsible, not grimly austere. And each needs trusted friends with whom to talk over difficult decisions about which steps are the right ones.

Paul says that in the church we are "members one of another." So it can be in such a supportive community.

CHAPTER 9

Reordering
Public Priorities

The church can play a key role in pointing the way to a hunger-free world, but that goal will not be reached unless U.S. political and economic institutions are persuaded to commit themselves more deliberately to its achievement. They control enormous amounts of money and have vast power over the attitudes and actions of Americans, and their policies affect the daily lives of countless millions around the world. Unfortunately, during the past decade the predominant impact of that influence has been to widen the gap between the poor and the affluent. We have invested far more in swords than in plowshares.

The church now must work in the political and economic arenas of this country to make this ominous record plainly evident and to point toward more responsible policies. Americans affirm that this is a "nation under God." The church has no more important task than to help decision-makers in government and industry take this claim seriously and discover its full implications for public policy and practice.

SIGNS OF RETREAT

Following the devastation of World War II the peoples of the world hoped that the nations would finally discover the ways that make for peace. Their hope was soon dimmed by the intense rivalry of the Cold War in which each of two armed camps sought to make itself stronger than the other. For the last thirty years increasingly more deadly weapons have been developed and increasingly large amounts spent for military purposes. The United States and the Soviet Union have led the way, but other nations—including many in the Third World—have entered the arms race. By 1975 the nations were spending about $275 billion annually for armaments. Their principal supplier was manufacturers in the United States. War—and preparation for it—had become lucrative business.

Even though the Vietnam War is over and the United States possesses extraordinary overkill capacity, our defense budget continues to spiral upward. In 1974 this nation spent $78 billion for defense and the following year $85 billion. For 1976 the Administration proposed a defense budget of $94 billion. Department of Defense projections call for a 13 percent average annual increase in expenditures between 1975 and 1980.

The enormity of these sums can be grasped by certain comparisons. For example, each billion dollars now spent for defense could be used to make 133,000 acres of idle river-basin land sufficiently productive to provide 1.1

million tons of rice annually for decades to come. For each acre put into productive use one family could be fed and employed. Two other comparisons: The U.S. defense budget devours an average of $246 million each day, but our government is proposing to give the World Food Council only $200 million for a whole year. In 16 hours our military establishment spends more than the World Health Organization and the Food and Agricultural Organization spend in a year.

As the amounts spent for defense have shot up, there has been a corresponding neglect of the poor in this nation and around the world. In spite of large amounts spent for federal food assistance programs, our nation's needy have become hungrier and poorer. In 1975 a Senate committee estimated that only 18 million of the 38 million undernourished U.S. citizens eligible to receive food stamps did so. Other far-reaching needs have remained inadequately faced. Among the nations of the world the United States ranks only 18th in doctor-patient ratio, 15th in literacy, 15th in infant mortality, and 26th in life expectancy. No other developed nation tolerates the kind of slums, the persistent unemployment, the lack of medical care, and the hunger that still characterize this country.

Even more striking has been the diminishing of our attention (along with the attention of other rich nations) to the needs of the Third World—precisely at the time that the poorer nations most need the kind of aid that would allow them to develop the processes and structures necessary to end hunger. Arthur Simon incisively summarizes the pertinent data:

It is a matter of some consequence . . . that, measured as a percentage of rich countries' total income, as well as in value to poor countries, official development assistance has steadily dropped for more than a decade. . . . Measured in assistance per person living in poor countries, development aid declined in real terms by 30 percent from 1963 to 1973. Further, in 1974 poor countries paid back $8.4 billion in debt retirement to donor nations—almost as much as they received in new assistance. Add to this the $20 billion trade deficit of non-oil-exporting poor countries in 1974, and the *rich nations* became net recipients of money from the poor ones."[1]

The United States, unfortunately, has led the way in this downward plunge. Our nation is not the Santa Claus for Third World nations that some believe. As measured by the percentage of Gross National Product spent for development assistance in 1975, the United States ranked 15th among the 17 major donor nations. U.S. development assistance amounted to only 1/5 of 1 percent of our GNP. Each American paid an average of $450 in taxes for defense, but only $6 for development assistance to Third World nations.

Our reduction of development aid for the hungry nations has been justified in some quarters by arguments bearing the terms "triage" and "lifeboat ethics." *Triage* refers to the battlefield medical policy of establishing priorities among three groups of casualties: those with minor wounds who can survive without immediate care;

those who can survive if given immediate care; and those hopeless cases on whom limited medical personnel and supplies should not be wasted.

Triage advocates say that hungry nations can be similarly divided and that our limited resources require us to make hard decisions about which nations should receive our aid and which not. Triagists admit that a nation's present and future ability to help the United States should enter into the decision about whether or not it will receive U.S. aid. According to their criteria, such nations as Bangladesh and India should receive no American aid. The moral act, say the triagists, is for us to concentrate our resources elsewhere and let nature take its grim course among the doomed nations.

According to the lifeboat ethicists, the affluent nations can be likened to people safely installed in lifeboats, while the poor nations are like desperate shipwreck victims swimming in the sea, all clamoring for a place in the lifeboats. Those in the boats have several choices, but the most prudent one is to keep the other people out, for if the boats are overfilled they will swamp and drown the privileged.

As increasing numbers of analysts have observed, triage and lifeboat theorists have received more attention than their arguments deserve, for their analogies are sloppily drawn and their reasoning overlooks elementary facts about the world situation. For instance, a country like Bangladesh, with numerous human and natural resources, cannot be compared to a mortally wounded man;

nor are the abundantly blessed affluent nations as helpless as medics on a battlefield. Similarly, the lifeboat theorists fail to recognize that our situation is more like that of an ocean liner whose relatively few first-class passengers persist in making life difficult for the large number of increasingly restive third-class passengers. The simplistic, self-serving content of these arguments is a warning to us of the numbness with which some Americans now react to the tragedy of world hunger, and the ease with which they rationalize their own inaction.

SIGNS OF PROMISE

To ignore such facts about the "state of the nation" would be to underestimate the difficulty of our task. But to end our analysis here would be to ignore other facts that constitute grounds for hope that the United States can commit more of its resources to the battle for a hunger-free world.

First, we must recognize the opportunity that our free nation gives citizens to work diligently for a change of national priorities. Every citizen has this right, and every Christian citizen has the urgent obligation to exercise this right fully. Moreover, many Christian laypersons hold jobs that give them influence upon the direction taken by American business. Many more—as well as numerous religious organizations—are stockholders in corporations. These are vitally important positions from which to seek to replace a ruthless "business is business" attitude with the recognition that "business is responsibility"—our economic institutions must seek a fair profit in ways that respect rather than exploit people and the earth.

Support for these critical tasks in government and business can be drawn from a discerning analysis of this nation's dominant traditions. Our past points the way toward action on behalf of the world's hungry. Through much of our national history we have acted aggressively to help overcome the forces that deny freedom. Critics are right in reminding us of the aggressiveness with which too often we have denied freedom to many. But that is not the mainstream of our national past. At our best we have acted upon the conviction, expressed in the Constitution, that the "blessings of liberty" are the right of all. Such conviction, President Lincoln rightly saw, gave hope to the world that "in due time the weights should be lifted from the shoulders of all men, and that all should have an equal chance."

Today those weights press heavily upon the human family. For half of the world's population they are experienced as crushing poverty, the most critical form of which is hunger. In recent years some of our political leaders have recognized that this nation's battle on behalf of freedom must become a battle against poverty and hunger. "A hungry man," said Adlai Stevenson in 1952, "is not a free man." The following year President Eisenhower eloquently articulated America's real power: "Every gun that is made, every warship launched, every rocket fired signifies, in the final sense, a theft from those who hunger and are not fed, those who are cold and not clothed. This is not a way of life at all . . . it is humanity hanging from a cross of iron." And in 1974 Secretary of State Kissinger, speaking on behalf of President Ford at the World Food Conference, proclaimed American willingness to join other nations in commitment to a bold objective: "that within a decade no child will go to bed hungry, that no family will fear for its next day's bread, and that no human being's future and capacities will be stunted by malnutrition."

Such vision receives more support from the American people today than is often realized. An extensive nationwide survey conducted in October 1972 revealed that 68 percent of the American public favored assistance to poor countries. Significantly, the survey showed that most Americans are not aware of the seriousness of world poverty, that most have an inflated idea of how much the United States spends for Third World development assistance, and that when people are provided with accurate data, their support for foreign economic assistance increases sharply. Similar findings were reported in September 1975 by a panel of eight major public opinion analysts who appeared before the Senate Foreign Relations Committee. They agreed that the American people are concerned about the decline of American prestige around the world, that they are ahead of most political leaders in recognizing the need for global economic interdependence, and that they are discontent with continued heavy reliance upon military means for achieving this nation's goals.

The American people are capable of responding to informed moral leadership that urges recovery of our nation's role as a wise champion of freedom and as a generous partner in the global battle against hunger.

The time is ripe for the churches to give such leadership.

THE WAY AHEAD

Some venturesome Christian pathfinders have moved into the political and economic arenas and are charting directions that can help all Christians find their way.

We should know something about several organizations whose work provides significant insight and stimulation for all Christians. Wherever possible, we should become directly involved in their programs.

The first one that we shall note is the Interreligious Taskforce on U.S. Food Policy. This is a Washington-based cooperative effort by representatives of twenty-two Protestant, Catholic, and Jewish bodies to influence federal policy on domestic and international food issues. The Taskforce has properly perceived that Christians must work ecumenically to achieve such large objectives and that they should not hesitate to move beyond the Christian camp to find like-minded and like-hearted colleagues.

Taskforce members together study pending legislation, determine the position they will recommend, and then work to see that their position is effectively urged upon Congress by constituents across the country and by Taskforce presentations to Congressional committees. Their incisive analyses of federal legislation is circulated widely through letters and various religious publications.

Here are highlights of Taskforce recommendations made in July 1975 regarding U.S. development aid.

(1) The United States should commit itself to providing at least 0.70 percent of its Gross National Product for official development assistance by 1980 and 1.00 percent by 1983, and should begin in Fiscal Year 1976 a systematic process for attaining that goal.

(2) An increasing proportion of U.S. development assistance should be channeled through multilateral organizations such as the United Nations, its specialized agencies, and various development banks.

(3) The primary consideration in determining how U.S. bilateral development aid is to be allocated should be the level of a nation's need, not its political orientation or perceived value to U.S. political and security interests.

(4) Aid should be channeled to projects which most directly benefit the neediest people within a country.

(5) Monies should be used to fund indigenous projects that utilize local leadership and personnel and show promise of eliminating poverty.

(6) U.S. development assistance should provide more grants in relation to loans.

(7) Development assistance legislation should be separated from military and security legislation, with the Agency for International Development devoted exclusively to development assistance and disaster relief, and not used to further U.S. strategic and military foreign policy.

(8) U.S. foreign policy as a whole and U.S. foreign aid in particular should be so reformed as to enhance, not interfere with, the self-development of nations, particularly their efforts to feed the hungry.

A second organization seeking a more responsible U.S. food policy is the Food Research and Action Center. It too is eager for its work to be known and utilized by churches across the country. FRAC is a church- and foundation-funded organization of attorneys and researchers which acts especially through legal channels on behalf of U.S. poor people who are struggling to eradicate hunger from their communities. Since its inception in 1970 FRAC has been in the forefront of efforts to make the federal government's food assistance programs more responsive to the needs of America's poor.

Among the major achievements of the organization have been three cases won in the U.S. Supreme Court that established important new rights for food stamp recipients; numerous court orders requiring the service of free school lunches to needy children in communities such as Philadelphia, Cleveland, Kansas City, Boston, Rochester, Las Vegas, and Little Rock; publication of the only book-length studies on the National School Breakfast Program and the Day Care Center Food Program which have revealed official efforts to block the growth of these essential anti-hunger programs and have called for steps to make these programs fully available to all the nation's poor children; and frequent testimony before Congressional committees documenting the shortcomings of federal and state efforts to end hunger in America.

A third organization working for a change in national priorities is the Interfaith Center on Corporate Responsibility. Related to the National Council of Churches, the ICCR is a coalition of twenty-five Protestant and Roman Catholic bodies concerned about the social implications of church investments in American business. The top priority of the Center now is research and action regarding the relation of large American corporations to world hunger. An example of that concern is the Center's investigation of the promotion by infant-milk companies of bottle feeding in the Third World. Encouragement of bottle feeding and discouragement of breast feeding is a serious source of malnutrition among low-income families in developing nations. The Center has initiated dialogue with three leading American manufacturers of infant-milk formula, and as a result of stockholder resolutions filed by ICCR member groups, two of the corporations have provided in-depth public reports about their infant-milk promotion and sales overseas. It remains to be seen what changes will be made in corporate policy, but at least the issue of social responsibility has been effectively raised.

The ICCR is also engaged in a wider program of research and action that includes an examination of major corporate landholders, a look at the fertilizer industry, and study of the relationship of U.S. corporations to the determination of U.S. food policy. The Center encourages local and regional groups around the country to make use of its monthly publication, the *Corporate Examiner*, in order to become informed about steps that can be taken to challenge American business to a greater awareness of its social responsibility.

The final group that we shall consider is Bread for the World, a rapidly growing Christian citizens' movement that since its inception in 1974 has enrolled approximately 12 thousand members across the country. A major objective of the organization is to form Bread for the World groups in local communities that will systematically present informed convictions about U.S. food policy to every member of Congress. A monthly newsletter analyzes current food issues facing Congress and the Administration. Seminars are held widely to help members reflect on their political responsibility in the light of the gospel and to provide necessary information for effective political action.

BFW's major program during the autumn months of 1975 reflected its fundamental objectives and patterns of operation. Members organized a nationwide Thanksgiving "offering of letters" first presented in churches during November, then forwarded by the thousands to members of Congress in support of a resolution already introduced in the Senate and House declaring that the right of every person to a nutritionally adequate diet is "henceforth to be recognized as a cornerstone of U.S. policy."

The key commitments called for in the "Resolution Declaring as National Policy the Right to Food" echoed central objectives of Bread for the World:

Resolved that it is the sense of the Senate and House of Representatives that

(1) Every person in this country and throughout the world has the right to food—the right to a nutritionally adequate diet—and that this right is henceforth to be recognized as a cornerstone of U.S. policy; and

(2) This right become a fundamental point of reference in the formation of legislation and administrative decision in areas such as trade, assistance, monetary reform, military spending, and all other matters that bear on hunger; and

(3) Concerning hunger in the United States we seek to enroll on food assistance programs all who are in need, to improve those programs to insure that recipients receive an adequate diet, and to attain full employment and a floor of economic decency for everyone; and

(4) Concerning global hunger this country increase its assistance for self-help development among the world's poorest people, especially in countries most seriously affected by hunger, with particular emphasis on increasing food production among the rural poor; and that development assistance and food assistance, including assistance given through private, voluntary agencies, increase over a period of years until such assistance has reached the target of one percent of our total national production (GNP).

Bread for the World's membership is committed to objectives that inevitably overlap with those of many other organizations addressing hunger issues. Several of those objectives that have not yet been discussed in this

116

chapter must now be mentioned, for they are critical to a comprehensive Christian strategy in the government and business arenas.

(1) *A U.S. food policy committed to world food security and rural development as proposed by the 1974 World Food Conference.* Among the steps necessary to implement this policy are U.S. participation in a world food reserve program, with reserves under national control; an increase in U.S. food assistance, especially the grant portion, to at least the level of 1/10 of this country's food exports, as our share toward the establishment of a grain reserve with an initial world target of 10 million tons; a substantial increase in the amount of food made available to the U.N. World Food Program; a fair return to the U.S. farmer for his production, with curbs against windfall profits, special measures to assist family farmers, and just wages for farm workers; and full U.S. participation in the International Fund for Agricultural Development, along with other steps to promote rural development in the poor countries by enabling them to secure adequate supplies of fertilizer and energy and by accelerating agricultural research that facilitates food production there.

(2) *Trade preferences for the poorest countries.* Trade is not perceived by the public as a hunger issue, but trade, even more than aid, vitally affects hungry people. These preferences should include lowering of trade barriers such as tariffs and quotas, especially on semi-processed and finished products (these barriers cost U.S. consumers perhaps as much as $10 to $15 billion annually); special

trade preference for the poorest countries which desperately need markets for their products if they are to work their way out of hunger; greatly increased planning for economic adjustment, including assistance for adversely affected U.S. workers and industries.

(3) *Efforts to deal with the population growth rate.* Only where social and economic gains include the poor, and where the rate of infant mortality begins to approximate that of the affluent nations, do people feel secure enough to limit family size. To help move toward such limitation of births the U.S. should expand efforts to enable the poor to work their way out of hunger and poverty; give additional assistance for health programs abroad aimed at reducing infant mortality and increasing health security; and provide additional support for research to develop family planning methods that are dependable, inexpensive, simple, safe, and morally acceptable to all.

Because Bread for the World stresses direct influence by Christian citizens upon the formulation of U.S. food policy, we shall look briefly at the efforts of one of its local chapters—this one organized in St. Joachim's Catholic parish in Philadelphia.

Since its beginning in late 1974 this group, numbering fifteen, has engaged in such activities as a food-stamp registration program, film-showing, sponsoring a Lenten prayer service within the parish, and sending petitions and letters to public officials on food-related issues. The group also puts out a mimeographed monthly newsletter to some four hundred persons, primarily in the parish.

In May 1975 representatives of the group visited their Congressman, William Green. Jack Hohenstein, chairman of St. Joachim's BFW group reports on what happened:

Our meeting with Congressman Green lasted well over an hour. We gave him an introduction to BFW and reviewed most of the "Right to Food" policy statement, urging him to study it carefully. Because he is chairman of the new sub-committee on trade of the House Ways and Means Committee, we discussed at some length the question of trade and the need to give trade preferences to the poorest countries, mentioning specifically the example of the European Common Market's agreement with 46 Less-Developed Countries in March. We agreed on the need for the government to protect the U.S. workers affected by changes in our trade policies.

We also agreed on the need for major reform and strengthening of the foreign aid program. . . . Mr. Green understood the need for the long-term consciousness-raising efforts of BFW, especially in the areas of excessive military spending and tax reform in which he has had long experience, and in the interrelatedness of such issues as food, pollution, war and peace, and the economy. He suggested the possibility of a meeting of church people in the Third Congressional District which we've since arranged for July 17. We agreed to keep in touch. He will keep us informed of the progress of legislation and offered the use of his Philadelphia-Washington direct phone line for urgent issues.

Christians in every community in this nation can, and should, follow the example of these pioneers. Through such efforts this nation can become a responsible partner in the battle against global hunger. It can happen! It must.

Epilogue:

The Future That Can Come

We are committed to achieving a world that is free of hunger. We know the enormous dimensions of the present crisis, and we know how little time is left for decisive action. Also we have some inkling of the holocaust that may overtake rich and poor alike if such action is not taken.

But what if the world does move immediately to bold, responsible action? What then might our global community look like by the end of this century?

As an agronomist and a theologian, we are soberly optimistic about the future that can come. We are not doomsday prophets. We are hopeful chiefly because God is committed to this end. Moreover, we know that the worldwide church has an enormous capacity for energizing the social processes that can help it to happen. Given these facts, and given the sufficiency of soil, adequate climate patterns, and the availability of agricultural abilities, energy, and imagination, as well as the yearning of nearly two billion people to break free from the shackles of hunger—we believe this future can come.

It can come if we develop carefully the remaining one-fifth of the earth's arable soil. It can come if we revolutionize temperate-zone agriculture so that it becomes dependent on solar energy instead of on fossil-fuel dependent technologies and economic structures requiring high production for high profits. A world without hunger can come if the nations' military budgets are reduced to make room for proper commitments to the conquest of hunger.

During the next two decades the now dependent food-deficit nations can become self-sufficient. When this future comes, each nation will produce food within the natural environmental capacities of its own lands. The vast natural energy resources of intensive, year-long sunlight and rainfall in the tropical world will be converted to enormous production levels of leguminous grasses for livestock—for milk, butter, cheese, and beef. Fiber, wood, and vegetable oil crops will continue in the tropical world. Livestock and plant diseases will be subdued. And the vast prairie lands of the world, where the soil is rich and deep, will produce our needed dietary budget of grains. Consumption patterns requiring large amounts of fiber, wood, vegetable oil, tobacco, sugar, rubber, coffee, and tea will be reduced in the rich world in order to make room for the production of food crops. The transition from "colonial crops" to food crops can be made in two decades.

Soil will be far better managed in every climate and on every continent. Dust storms will diminish, as will their

121

effect on our global climatic patterns. Rivers will cease to run red with the eroded soil that now settles on shrimp beds and plugs the world's estuaries—the cradles of the fish of the sea. Rural communities will come alive, and migration to the cities as a final and desperate lunge for survival will end. Creative employment will exist for all, across all the lands. The violence of hunger, famine, landlessness, high infant mortality rates, and short life-span will dissipate; so will the need for armies and police states.

"Some dream dreams and say 'why?' Others dream and say 'why not?'" This future can come. It requires trust, sacrifice, hope, and love. God speaks to us out of the misery of his people, just as he spoke to Moses: "Go. Set my people free!"

Notes

1. The Deadly but Conquerable Foe

1. Alan Berg, *The Nutrition Factor* (Washington, D.C.: Brookings Institution, 1973), p. 9.
2. *Time*, November 11, 1974, p. 68. Reprinted by permission from *Time*, The Weekly Newsmagazine; Copyright Time Inc.
3. A summary analysis of how that money could be creatively used is in Larry Minear, *New Hope for the Hungry?* (New York: Friendship Press, 1975), pp. 74-75.

2. Causes of Hunger

1. William Rich, *Smaller Families through Social and Economic Progress* (Washington, D.C.: Overseas Development Council), Monograph No. 7, January 1973, p. 76.
2. John Gardner, *The Recovery of Confidence* (New York: W. W. Norton, 1970), pp. 84-85.

4. God's Generosity and Our Responsibility

1. Joachim Jeremias, *The Prayers of Jesus* (Naperville, Ill.: Allenson, 1967), p. 94.

6. Heightening Awareness

1. John Kenneth Galbraith, *The Affluent Society* (New York: New American Library, 1958), p. 144.
2. E. F. Schumacher, *Small Is Beautiful* (Torchbooks; New York: Harper, 1974), p. 94.

7. Mobilizing Church Resources

1. Richard K. Taylor, *Economics and the Gospel* (Philadelphia: United Church Press, 1973), pp. 112, 113.

8. Developing Responsible Lifestyles

1. Cited in John Taylor, *Enough Is Enough* (Naperville, Ill.: SCM Book Club, 1975), p. 20.

9. Reordering Public Priorities

1. Arthur Simon, *Bread for the World* (Grand Rapids: Eerdmans, and Paramus, N.J.: Paulist Press, 1975), p. 112.

Resources for Study and Action

1. BOOKS

A. General Problem Descriptions

Bickel, Lennard. *Facing Starvation: A Biography of Dr. Norman E. Borlaug.* New York: Reader's Digest Press, 1974.

Brown, Lester. *By Bread Alone.* New York: W. W. Norton, 1974.

Simon, Arthur. *Bread for the World.* Grand Rapids: Eerdmans, and Paramus, N.J.: Paulist Press, 1975.

The United Nations World Food Conference: Assessment of the World Food Situation, Present and Future. Rome, November 5-16, 1974.

B. Nutritional Aspects

Berg, Alan. *The Nutritional Factor: Its Role in National Development.* Washington, D.C.: Brookings Institution, 1973.

Serban, George, ed. *Nutrition and Mental Functions.* New York: Plenum Press, 1975.

C. Background Studies

Barnet, Richard J., and Muller, Ronald E. *Global Reach: The Power of Multinational Corporations.* New York: Simon and Schuster,1974.

Borgstrom, George. *The Hungry Planet: The Modern World at the Edge of Famine,* 2nd rev. ed. New York: Macmillan, 1972.

Brown, Lester, and Finsterbush, Gail W. *Man and His Environment: Food.* New York: Harper, 1972.

Campbell, Rex R., and Wade, Jerry L., eds. *Society and Environment: The Coming Collision.* Boston: Allyn and Bacon, 1972.

Cochrane, Willard. *The World Food Problem: A Guardedly Optimistic View.* New York: T. Y. Crowell, 1969.

Connelly, Philip, and Perlman, Robert. *The Politics of Scarcity: Resource Conflicts in International Relations.* New York: Oxford University Press, 1975.

Dumont, Rene, and Rosier, Bernard. *The Hungry Future.* New York: Praeger, 1969.

Elliott, Charles. *Patterns of Poverty in the Third World: A Study of Social and Economic Stratification.* New York: Praeger, 1975.

Ford Foundation (Energy Policy Project). *A Time to Choose: America's Energy Future.* Cambridge: Ballinger Publishing Co., 1974.

Gourou, Pierre. *The Tropical World: Its Social and Economic Conditions and Its Future Status,* 4th ed. New York: Halsted Press, 1974.

Heilbroner, Robert. *An Inquiry into the Human Prospect.* New York: W. W. Norton, 1974.

Makhijani, Arjun, and Poole, Alan. *Energy and Agriculture in the Third World.* Cambridge: Ballinger Publishing Co., 1975.

Meadows, Donella H., *et al. The Limits to Growth: A Report for the Club of Rome's Project on the Predicament of Mankind.* New York: Universe Books, 1972.

Mesarovic, Mihaljo, and Pestel, Edward. *Mankind at the Turning Point.* New York: New American Library, 1976.

Paddock, William and Paul. *Famine: 1975!* Boston: Little, Brown, 1968.

Rich, William. *Smaller Families Through Social and Economic Progress.* Washington, D.C.: Overseas Development Council, Monograph No. 7, Jan. 1973.

Schumacher, E. F. *Small Is Beautiful: A Study of Economics as if People Mattered.* Torchbooks; New York: Harper, 1974.

Tydings, Joseph D. *Born to Starve.* New York: Morrow, 1970.

Wharton, Clifton. *The Green Revolution: Cornucopia or Pandora's Box.* Foreign Affairs Report, 1969.

D. *Biblical, Ethical and Theological Studies*

Batey, Richard. *Jesus and the Poor.* New York: Harper, 1972.

Cochrane, Arthur C. *Eating and Drinking with Jesus: An Ethical and Biblical Inquiry.* Philadelphia: Westminster Press, 1974.

Derr, Thomas S. *Ecology and Human Need.* Philadelphia: Westminster Press, 1975.

Dickinson, Richard. *To Set at Liberty the Oppressed.* Geneva: World Council of Churches, 1975.

Goulet, Denis. *The Cruel Choice.* New York: Atheneum, 1973.

Gutierrez, Gustavo. *A Theology of Liberation.* Maryknoll, N. Y.: Orbis Books, 1972.

Hengel, Martin. *Property and Riches in the Early Church.* Philadelphia: Fortress Press, 1975.

Imsland, Donald. *Celebrate the Earth.* Minneapolis: Augsburg Publishing House, 1971.

Koyama, Kosuke. *Waterbuffalo Theology.* Maryknoll, N.Y.: Orbis, 1974.

Minear, Larry. *New Hope for the Hungry?* New York: Friendship Press, 1975.

Minear, Paul S. *I Pledge Allegiance: Patriotism and the Bible.* Philadelphia: Geneva Press, 1975.

Taylor, John V. *Enough Is Enough.* Naperville, Ill.: SCM Book Club, 1975.

Westerman, Claus. *Creation.* Philadelphia: Fortress Press, 1974.

Yoder, John Howard. *The Politics of Jesus.* Grand Rapids: Eerdmans, 1972.

2. ADDRESSES

Alternatives, 701 North Eugene Street, Greensboro, N.C. 27401.

Bread for the World, 235 East 49th Street, New York, N.Y. 10017.

Church World Service, 475 Riverside Drive, New York, N.Y. 10027.

CROP, Box 968, Elkhart, IN 46514.

5-C Co-op, 748 East Epworth Avenue, Cincinnati, OH 45232.

Food Research and Action Center, 25 West 43rd Street, New York, N.Y. 10036.

Interfaith Center on Corporate Responsibility, 475 Riverside Drive, New York, N.Y. 10027.

Interreligious Taskforce on U.S. Food Policy, 110 Maryland Avenue, N.E., Washington, D.C. 20002.

United Methodist Committee on Relief, 475 Riverside Drive, New York, N.Y. 10027.

3. AUDIO-VISUAL RESOURCES

"A World Hungry," a five-unit filmstrip series based on the work of C. Dean Freudenberger: (1) "You may have heard: Fictions and facts about world hunger"; (2) "How hunger happens: A galaxy of causes"; (3) "The green counterrevolution: Plans for justice"; (4) "Knowledge and lifestyle: A personal response"; (5) "Churches and political action: More personal responses." TeleKETICS, 1229 South Santee Street, Los Angeles, CA 90015.

Beyond the Next Harvest. Film, color, 30 mins. Mass-Media Ministries, 2116 N. Charles St., Baltimore, MD 2128.

Bread for the World. Filmstrip. Bread for the World, 235 East 49th Street, New York, N.Y. 10017.

Sahel: Border of Hell. Film, 50 mins. Post-Newsweek, New York, N.Y.

Hunger. Film, animated, color, 11 mins. The Learning Corporation of America, 711 Fifth Avenue, New York, NY 10022.

The Global City. Filmstrip and media kit. Institute for the Study of Peace, St. Louis University, St. Louis, MO.

Tilt. Film, color, animated, 19 mins. Film Board of Canada. Distributed by CRM Educational Films, Delmar, CA 92014.